D0093183

Donald O. Clifton, Ph.D. (1924–2003)

The Father of Strengths-Based Psychology and
Creator of the Clifton StrengthsFinder®

The Clifton StrengthsFinder is the culmination of more than 50 years of
Dr. Donald O. Clifton's lifelong work: leading millions of people around the
world to discover their strengths. In 2002, Dr. Clifton was honored by an
American Psychological Association Presidential Commendation as
the Father of Strengths-Based Psychology.

Teach
With Your
Strengths

How Great Teachers Inspire Their Students

By Rosanne Liesveld and Jo Ann Miller
with Jennifer Robison

Gallup Press, New York

GALLUP PRESS
1251 Avenue of the Americas
23rd Floor
New York, NY 10020

Library of Congress Control Number: 2005924914
ISBN 1-59562-006-0

10 9 8 7

Gallup®, Clifton StrengthsFinder™ and the 34 Clifton StrengthsFinder theme
names, Gallup Press™, Gallup University™, and StrengthsFinder® are
trademarks of The Gallup Organization, Princeton, NJ. All other trademarks are
property of their respective owners.

This book is dedicated to my mother, Opal Kats, a country schoolteacher, who lived and loved greatness in teaching. And to my new grandson, Johnny, who deserves the very best teachers in the world.

— Rosanne

To all great teachers everywhere, but especially to Don Clifton, the ultimate teacher. People will be learning from him forever.

— Jo Ann

Contents

IMPORTANT

Your ID code is located in the insert in the back of this book. Use your ID code to log on to the Clifton StrengthsFinder Web site and take the Clifton StrengthsFinder assessment.

GO TO:

sf1.strengthsfinder.com

Introduction

Every survey conducted since 1968 by Phi Delta Kappa (PDK), the professional organization for educators, has shown that Americans worry about a lack of great teachers — as well they should. Teachers have a greater effect on students, and ultimately our society, than anyone other than parents.

Teachers are so important that, for decades, The Gallup Organization has directed the best minds in education and psychology to study, interview, analyze, and decode what makes a teacher great. The research turned up a mountain of useful information. It also revealed this stunning fact: All great teachers are alike in a key way — they use their natural talents to the utmost, whether they are aware of it or not. What's more, great teachers don't waste time on their weaknesses if those weaknesses don't interfere with their teaching, although they do manage weaknesses if they must. When good teachers understand their talents, then build on those talents to create strengths, they become even better with students. That's what this book is all about.

When you were learning to be a teacher, you were taught a lot of things. You excelled at some of them and struggled with others. Naturally, you preferred to focus on the areas in which you excelled. What sane person wouldn't?

However, someone undoubtedly told you that to be a really good teacher, you had to concentrate on those things that came harder to you — things that you liked less and that you didn't do well. The theory is that the easy stuff will take care of itself, so you need to concentrate your effort on improving your areas of weakness. You need to become more "well-rounded."

Well, this theory is counterproductive, and worse, it can be destructive. "Fixing" your weaknesses simply doesn't work; at best, if you work really hard with great devotion, you can become mediocre in those areas. In the meantime, because attempts to fix weaknesses distract attention and effort from what you naturally do well, you squander the opportunity to be great. This is a real problem because, frankly, America needs great teachers.

More than a job, teaching is a calling, and teaching with strengths helps educators fulfill the mission of that calling. Indeed, teaching with strengths makes teachers happier, more productive, likelier to stay in the field, and far more successful in the classroom — thus helping more students learn and grow. In the 2002 Phi Delta Kappa/ Gallup study, Rose and Gallup (2002) found that 73% of Americans said that one of the most serious problems facing education is a lack of good teachers. What Americans aren't aware of is that thousands of teachers are letting their greatest talents go to waste and busily attending to their weaknesses. As a result, generations of students are being taught by teachers who are struggling to be well-rounded instead of maximizing their talents.

It doesn't have to be this way. Decades of research have proven that talents are extremely powerful, and the influence of teaching with strengths on students has a dramatic long-term effect. The problem is that teachers haven't had the practical tools they need to use what the scientists have discovered about strengths.

That changes with this book. Inside, you'll gain key insights from the research, visit with teachers in the classroom, see what they've revealed in structured interviews, and learn the difference between average teachers and outstanding teachers. Most importantly, you'll discover your own talents as a teacher and how to unleash them.

Chapter One

The Unorthodox Behavior
of Great Teachers

Teachers' influence on students is second only to that of their parents. Indeed, as the majority of Americans end their formal education when they're seniors in high school, and sometimes earlier (only about a third of Americans graduate from college), most of us have left formal education forever by the time we're 18. So clearly, the responsibility for educating our society rests almost entirely with elementary and secondary school teachers. Simply put, we need them to be great.

The first thing to know about great teachers is that they are, in the best way, unorthodox. Great teachers' methods and intuitions are different. They don't operate like other teachers, and they don't believe everything they're taught or told. They work by instinct more than even they know, having worked out the strategies and approaches that succeed for them in reaching different students. In an extraordinarily high number of cases, their instincts lead them to the results they want — better educated students.

Fred, a teacher in New York state, is one example of a great teacher who takes an unorthodox approach. "There was no question whatsoever about hugging a child, even a crying child," he says. "You had to be standoffish. But there were times — well, I just didn't care. Even though I knew I could be brought up on charges for hugging a crying child, I just said it'd be worth it. That kid's really hurting."

Instinctively, Fred could not tolerate doing the "right thing" because it meant, in reality, doing the wrong thing — alienating a child from his teacher and ultimately, his education. In the end, as with other great teachers you'll read about in this book, Fred's unorthodox approach is exactly right for the situations he faces. Great teachers do what Fred does — the right thing at the right time. It's not the result of training or education, it occasionally courts trouble, and great teachers almost always say it was worth it.

Innate Talent for the Job

What separates great teachers like Fred from the pack? Four decades of research, including Gallup's interviews with thousands of educators, offer some compelling insights. The overarching theme of the results is that great teachers have something that less effective teachers don't have — innate talent for the job. That talent is natural and individual, and it spurs great teachers to behave in ways unique to them.

Just as great teachers are different from the pack, and even different from each other in many ways, they share several important commonalities. One of them is that they recognize that some of what they've been taught about teaching is misinformation.

Teaching Misinformation

Great teachers know that a lot of what they've learned about teaching is tremendously useful, but some of it isn't, and they can tell the difference. The distinction is important. Operating from poor assumptions about education and student behavior can undermine learning, poison spirits, and encourage students to tune out, sometimes permanently. In fact, interviews with educators have uncovered two essential feelings common to great teachers: One is love — love of students, learning, and teaching. The other, which is no surprise, is exasperation with educational nonsense — conventional wisdom about teaching that is, in fact, misinformation. So what misinformation do great teachers reject? Read on.

"Some students are inherently lazy, rebellious, or difficult"

The National Education Association's (NEA) survey, *Status of the American Public School Teacher 2000-2001*, asked teachers if they intended to stay in the profession, and if not, why. Of those who said they will leave teaching if they can, 57% said working conditions and low salaries will drive them out, 8% said it's the administration, and 5% said they couldn't stand the parents. Only 4% said their desire to leave teaching is related to their students. However, in the 2002 Phi Delta Kappa/Gallup survey, 76% of American adults said that lack of student discipline is a serious problem facing schools. (Rose and Gallup, 2002) Many teachers reported that social standards and manners are not what they once were, but they don't accept the notion that young people are inherently bad.

Clearly, there's conflicting information. A lot of people seem to think that young people are just plain troublesome. Darcy, a kindergarten teacher, says, "People are always asking me, 'How can you do it day in and day out?' I say, 'You just don't understand!' The look on my kids' faces when something clicks, when they finally get it — it's completely worth everything you do."

Students are not prisoners or employees. Teachers with little talent for the job assume that they're working with a captive audience that must follow orders, but they're wrong. The state may require young people to attend school until the age of 16, but no one can force someone to learn. Students are essentially volunteers, and great teachers know that students must be emotionally engaged to learn effectively. Emotional engagement is a process, and it starts with a psychological connection. That connection can't be mandated. Fortunately, young people are innately curious — and curiosity is the first step toward that connection.

Young people who are disengaged won't work hard, which is why they get labeled as lazy. Sometimes these students get so bored or are so far behind that they act out, and they're called rebellious. Some young people are so disengaged in class that they refuse to cooperate at all, and that, of course, makes them difficult. Joanna, a high school English and Spanish teacher, points out, "You hear all the time that kids are lazy. But what a lot of people fail to realize is that many of those [high school age] kids work. They show up for their job shift at 3:30 on the dot and work until close — 10:00, 11:00, midnight — sometimes even later. Of course they don't want to do anything; they're exhausted. And the kids who don't work? A lot of them never learned basic skills early on. They do nothing because they can't do anything."

Great teachers know that it's harder to reach some students than others. But they also know, instinctively, that it's possible to engage almost any young person. As Gail, a teacher, puts it, "It takes a good teacher to make good students." Particularly resourceful teachers know that if they can get the least compliant and hardest to engage young people on their side first, the rest of the class will follow. These teachers don't coerce, force, or trick students. Instead, they tap students' innate interests and needs to help them learn, which has a side effect of building caring relationships between students and teachers.

Winning over noncompliant students is tremendously rewarding. Over and over again, great teachers admit that they enjoy the challenging students most. "I'm particularly attracted to the ones who are going off the path a little bit, not able to focus, who can't listen or be disciplined in other places," says Vickie, a California teacher. "Underneath all that is something very special. They seem to do well with me." Denise, a teacher from Texas, shares this sentiment: "I'm mostly motivated by the students who seem to really have the potential, but for some reason, they're not using it. To me, there's something missing right there, and if you find that one little piece, they can become compliant, motivated students." Jackie, an eighth-grade teacher from Tennessee, puts it bluntly: "I think I go for the noncompliant ones because I like the challenge."

The fact is that all human beings need stimulation. No one is happy staring at a wall for eight hours. Everyone is naturally inclined to learn, especially between the ages of 1 and 25, when, as new neurological research shows, our brains are developing neural pathways and connections that we will use for the rest of our lives. Great teachers use their students' needs, interests, and curiosities and turn them toward the curricula — "captivating them, not entertaining them," as one teacher puts it. Not everyone can do this. But great teachers do it so naturally that they often aren't even aware they are doing it. That's why exceptional teachers are offended by the lazy/rebellious/difficult labels that people hang on noncompliant students. Labeling a young person as difficult is essentially writing him or her off, and great teachers try and try again, refusing to give up on students.

"Anyone can teach"

Teaching demands talents for teaching — natural abilities that require cultivation and hard work to master. Assuming that anyone can teach breeds mediocrity, just as surely as thinking that anyone can be a doctor, architect, or police officer would foster unremarkable performance in those professions.

This assumption is bad for students, and it's not particularly helpful for teachers, either. The not-so-good teachers spend their careers trying to do something at which they won't ever excel, that never gets easier, and that is increasingly less rewarding. And the exceptional teachers are often forced to compromise what they know is right to fit in with the pack. What's more, the outstanding teachers rarely get the recognition they deserve, and they are pressured to assume models that aren't meant for them — models that lead to mediocrity.

Thinking that teaching requires no more innate ability than driving a car or making toast leads to mediocre educational standards. That leads to mediocre teachers and mediocre, or worse, students. Great teachers resent that. "It happens all the time," says one veteran teacher. "You don't have much choice. You have to do what you're told, but it makes us resentful. You go along, thinking maybe it will work out. You just do the best you can with what you have to do. That's why I want to move to administration. Some of us have even talked about starting our own school where we can teach the way we know we should."

"The more education or experience, the better the teacher"

The first two years or so of a teacher's career provide constant education in what they didn't cover in college about real-world teaching. That's why it's tempting to turn to more experienced teachers for guidance. Indeed, some teachers have found that their professional lifelines are experienced educators, and those beloved mentors help a lot of people become great teachers. But not every seasoned teacher is so helpful. Some, mercifully few, are flat-out discouraging to new teachers and less-than-stellar in the classroom.

It can be disappointing to find out that seniority doesn't necessarily equal excellence, but it's true nonetheless. Experience doesn't translate into exceptional job performance in teaching or in any other field. There's a reason for that — the positive effects of experience on job performance wear off pretty quickly. In fact, in most professions, they wear off in five years.

Meta-analysis, the mathematical and statistical study of the combined results of several studies, has uncovered the five-year fade-out effect. That is, someone who has been teaching for six years has all the benefits of experience, as they relate to job performance, that a 30-year teaching veteran possesses. Speaking about job performance across most fields, Frank Schmidt, Ph.D., one of the world's leading meta-analysts, says:

> Initial learning on the job is pretty steep during the first five years. . . . people have learned about as much as they are going to learn about how to do that job after the fifth year. The difference you can attribute to experience will fade away and will no longer affect performance. What will become important will be mental ability, personality, and conscientiousness — personality traits. These traits do not fade away. That is, their predictive ability [for job performance] continues. (Schmidt, 2004)

It's the people with the personality traits for the job who keep getting better, year after year. Some teachers have the right personality traits — and some don't, no matter how long they've been in the classroom. That's why some veterans of education are so helpful to young teachers and students and some aren't.

Unfortunately, many teachers never realize that experience and talent are two different things. The fact is, young people don't respond to seniority or post-graduate degrees. They respond to teachers who have passion for their work. And people who don't have talent for teaching soon lose whatever passion they had. The NEA survey, *Status of the American Public School Teacher 2000-2001*, asked teachers why they stay in the field, and 30% said they had "too much invested to leave now." Twenty-one percent said that if they had the choice to make again, they wouldn't choose to become teachers. Some of this reflects, as the NEA noted, "individual maturation and changing needs." Whatever the explanation, this doesn't bode well for students.

Dan Goldhaber, Ph.D., a senior research associate at the Urban Institute, has found that only 3% of "the contribution teachers made to student learning" could be connected to experience and education. He states:

> The measures of teacher quality that are used by most public school systems to screen candidates and determine compensation — certification, experience, and education level — have been well researched, but there is little definitive empirical evidence that these characteristics, defined in general terms, are associated with higher student achievement. Teachers' educational levels appear to make a difference when the education is related to the subject taught, but advanced degrees do not appear to serve as a good measure of quality in general. There is also some evidence that experienced teachers are more effective with students, but the benefits of additional years of experience appear to level off early in a teacher's career. Measures of teachers' academic skills, such as their verbal ability, may more accurately predict their effectiveness, but there is far less evidence on this

issue, and these findings are also not conclusive. There is little evidence on the issue of teacher certification as well, and the evidence that does exist is mixed. (Goldhaber, 2002)

So educator experience has less influence on students than simple good teaching. The masters of science degrees that half of all teachers have earned are less important to students than they are to the people who hold them. One caveat: Though advanced degrees may not have much effect on student achievement, many teachers find them personally rewarding, though expensive (on average, teachers spend $2,937 a year on their advanced education).

Learning more about the work you love is always beneficial, and higher education certainly has professional benefits — 48% of teachers say that they earn more money by getting more licenses and certifications. And of course, it's always nice to spend time with colleagues who are as excited about teaching as you are. Just don't expect higher education to turn a mediocre teacher into a great one. It doesn't work that way.

"Keep a professional distance"

"How you relate is everything," says Mary Beth, a high school principal. "When I started teaching twenty-eight years ago, the idea was: 'I don't care if they don't like me, as long as they learn.' We had all kinds of notions of rigor and not letting our guard down. Since then, I've come full circle and realized that relationships are what make the learning experience go."

Many great teachers find the image of the hardened disciplinarian disturbing, if not distressing. The get-tough approach suggests that students lie in wait, like half-starved pumas, for a moment of pedagogical weakness, then leap out and ravage any hope of learning — and teachers had better keep beating the kids back into the tall weeds or lose authority forever.

Teachers who employ the give-an-inch-they'll-take-a-mile method of teaching use threats to coerce respect because they can't earn it. This method is the result of poor classroom management, fear of losing control, and sometimes — though mercifully rarely — accumulated hostility toward students.

Punishment kills learning, and punishing eventually corrodes teachers. As Jane, a teacher in a big-city junior high, puts it: "Learning is fundamentally an act of self-confidence." There's a time and a place for getting tough, of course, but there's a difference between hard and soft control. Prison guards exert hard control. Great teachers master the softer variety. Ken, a high school English teacher, sets the tone of soft control on the very first day of class. "I tell them they count, they matter, they are of infinite value — and that's not negotiable, not in the classroom or out of it. Young people are thirsty for a caring adult. If you exhibit that you care about your students, they'll come to you. You'll have to peel them off you like Velcro."

Ken touches on an essential truth about teaching that Mary Beth alluded to earlier: It's all about relationships. The first thing great teachers do to create relationships is *give respect to students to earn respect from them*. Great teachers know that respect has to be earned because respect is not a quality that can be assigned. Furthermore, students have to respect their teachers before they can respect themselves and believe their work in school is important. As one teacher says, "Kids can spot fakers and posers instantly. They don't see why they should listen to you if you don't really care about them."

Great teachers win students over, sometimes subtly, sometimes actively. But they always do it by building positive, not punitive, relationships. The obvious tools of relationship building include memorizing names, learning students' personal interests and using them as a hook for learning, and making time for one-on-one discussions. High school students have the same basic need for relationships with teachers as do younger students. Every student needs real human interaction to excel. What's true for young people is also true for adults: Gallup's extensive research on employee engagement finds that adults seek workplaces where their managers care about them and in which their opinions count.

"Set high expectations"

Great teachers don't set high expectations. This might come as a surprise. Rather, great teachers set the *right* expectations for each student. Talented teachers have an innate sense of what those expectations should be.

One urban elementary school teacher relates, "If children set the outcomes that they want to attain, then my primary responsibility is to help them master those activities they need to reach that outcome. They don't always have the loftiest goal, but they've set a goal for themselves. And for them, that's important. If they believe that they are capable of doing something far greater, they will do it."

Every teacher must set and enforce some basic rules: come to class on time, be prepared, pay attention, participate. But beyond rules are expectations, which more directly relate to what students can achieve. Assuming that a C math student will get an A on the next report card is a high expectation. The right expectation might be that, with coaching and specific homework activities, he'll have long division down by November and bring the grade up to a B. Another high expectation is that a student who can't run around the block without lying down will win the Phys. Ed. Olympics. The right expectation might be that she'll get more exercise at home and improve her speed by 20%. A high expectation is a hope. The right expectation is a plan.

The problem with high expectations is that they can be mistaken for impossible standards, even by educators, and especially by students. Rather than inspiring students to greatness or encouraging them to achieve, those impossible expectations doom students to failure. This approach is hardly conducive to learning, and it can erode young students' self-esteem. As they get older, some students stop trying to meet impossibly high expectations, which can mean that they've given up trying to win their teacher's approval. Worse yet, teachers tell us, some students stop being able to recognize the difference between exorbitant expectations and ones that are within their reach. At that point, every lofty expectation looks impossible.

Low expectations are just as damaging. In some cases, low expectations are thought to boost self-esteem because they provide successes. But after the first couple of successes, even young people recognize hollow victories when they see them. Low expectations suggest, however subtly, that students aren't capable of doing better. Low expectations stall students and don't help them stretch or exceed their present abilities by developing new ones. Such expectations only inspire mediocrity. "That's why I hate 'teaching to the test,'" says one teacher. "It doesn't give kids any incentive to gain more than minimal competencies."

In 1968, a Harvard professor of social psychology, Dr. Robert Rosenthal, conducted a study on the effect of expectations. He and his team gave 650 students in a Chicago elementary school an IQ test ("The Harvard Test of Inflected Acquisition") at the beginning of the school year. The teachers were told that the test predicted "intellectual blooming" and indicated which students would have "surprising gains in intellectual competence." The teachers were given the names of students who the test identified as "potential bloomers" — about 20% of them. The teachers were told to look for dramatic intellectual growth in these young people, and like all good teachers, they encouraged growth when they found it.

The students were retested at the end of the semester and again at the end of the school year. The results were remarkable. The potential bloomers and the ordinary students improved their total, verbal, and reasoning IQ scores. But 47% of the potential bloomers gained 20 or more points, whereas only 19% of the other students did.

Here's the astounding part: The test never indicated anything; it had no predictive value at all. The students who were initially labeled as "bloomers" had been chosen at random. The only difference in intellectual possibility on the group level was a year's worth of the right expectations and some end-of-year test scores. Dr. Rosenthal calls this "the Pygmalion effect" because the students, clearly, were what their teachers made them. (Rosenthal, 1998) Expectations are important, and the right expectations for an individual student are critical.

"Public praise gives students a big head, and public rebukes keep them in line"

Great teachers love to see young people learn. They get very real and personal satisfaction out of student success — and happily voice that satisfaction in class. "You build on their small and big successes, and you build on their strengths. When you point out what they're doing well, they do that much better," says Sheila, a 35-year teaching veteran in an elementary school.

Recognition is neither benign nor destructive. Indeed, recognition is a powerful motivator, more so when given publicly, and especially when it's presented for an achievement of which the student is truly proud. Good teachers know that recognizing a 100% on a math test for a student who usually gets 100% isn't as meaningful as recognizing an 87% on a spelling test for a student who usually gets a 70%. (Of course, the tactful way to recognize the achievement is pointing out the 17 percentage point increase, not the grades.) Sadly, some students don't have glorious moments of high achievement very often. But great teachers recognize the success that's specific to the student, regardless of class comparison, and celebrate it.

Rose, a music teacher, realized one day that the only time some young people hear applause for themselves is during music programs. That applause, of course, was meant for the group, not individuals. "So I set about finding ways to make sure each student, somehow, got real applause for something he or she did," Rose says. "I wanted every one of my kids to be applauded for something, and when I actively looked for reasons, I found them. It made a big difference to them, I think."

Research shows that the more public the praise, the better. Eighty years ago, a researcher named Dr. Elizabeth Hurlock conducted a study with fourth- and sixth-grade math students. (Hurlock, 1925) She divided the students into four groups (we'll call them Groups A, B, C, and D) based on the results of a math test given on the first day of the experiment. All the groups took equally difficult math tests every day for five days. Each day, before the test papers were handed out, the students in Group A were identified by name and praised for the excellence of their work on the previous day and encouraged in front of the whole class. The students in Group B were also identified by name and criticized for their poor work, also in front of the entire class. Group C was totally ignored, although those students were present when Group A was praised and when Group B was criticized. Group D was the control group. They didn't hear anything about their grades or anyone else's. After the first test, they were separated from the other groups, and they took their tests on the four remaining days in a separate room.

Groups A and B improved their scores dramatically on the second day of testing, while Groups C and D didn't show significant improvement. By the third day, something dramatic happened. The scores of Group A got even better, and that improvement was sustained through the final test. As it turned out, Group A showed an overall improvement of 71%. Group B showed an overall improvement of only 19%. And the ignored students in Groups C? They showed a mere 5% overall improvement. In this study at least, public praise accounted for an amazing 66 percentage point difference in improvement.

"A magic curriculum, method, or theory will work for everyone"

Teachers have been burned before. Sometimes they find themselves just finishing the (mandated) implementation of one "brilliant" method when the next one comes along. Veteran educators have seen such curricula and methods come and go, some lingering, some dismissed as soon as they arrive. At the next retirement party, ask the exiting teacher which method or mandate worked best. Odds are, he or she won't be able to name one but may have a good story of frustration and aggravation to tell you.

The reason great teachers think the "magic method" is nonsense is because they know that every student is different and learns differently. Fortunately, human brains are similar enough that education doesn't have to be reinvented for each child. But no single method can accommodate the differences in the aggregate and yet speak to the differences in every individual.

Furthermore, "magic methods" don't, and can't, account for the differences among teachers. What may work beautifully for one teacher one year may not work with the next class — and may never work for another teacher ever. Seth, a middle school teacher in Nebraska, swears by cartooning. He explains, "I have boxes with pictures of stick people in them. The kids fill in the thought bubbles. It lets them write instead of verbalizing, which is easier for some kids." This method works great for Seth, but it wouldn't necessarily work for other teachers.

Ken, the master of soft control, depends on what he calls "cheap theatrics." He says, "When Caesar was killed, I stabbed myself with a cardboard sword. I flash the lights when there's a storm in the novel. The other day, I found myself standing on the desk. I didn't plan to stand on the desk when I got up that morning, but it occurred to me that if I enacted what happened to Dimsdale in *The Scarlet Letter*, they might get it, might get hooked." To be sure, every one of Ken's students was riveted, but a lot of other educators would feel like idiots enacting *The Scarlet Letter* from atop their desks. Different methods work for different teachers; different methods work for different students.

That's why great teachers "cherry pick" among the theories, methods, and curricula as much as they are permitted. They take what looks productive and leave the rest. Mary Beth, with 28 years of experience in the classroom and in administration, says, "The best instructors give choices. They let kids use their talents. The best teachers know that learning isn't the same for everybody." This might be one of the best arguments for post-graduate education for teachers. Higher education for teachers improves student learning by only 3%, but it does introduce teachers to interesting and useful new ideas that they may not have encountered otherwise.

"Teachers must love all students all the time"

The idea that any rational adult would beam with love at a child in the midst of his third outburst that day is unrealistic. Most great teachers, however, say that they really love their students — just not every single minute.

The vast majority of teachers — 73% according to the NEA survey *Status of the American Public School Teacher 2000-2001* — got into the field "to work with young people." But when great teachers say they want to work with young people, they really aren't talking about young people per se. There are lots of ways to work with young people that don't require years of college education and relatively low pay. In fact, though great teachers tend to like young people a lot, what they really love are learners. They love being part of someone's development. They love knowing that they played a significant part in someone's life. They love being remembered for their contributions to education. Great teachers respect and admire students for the work they do. They become teachers for the young people but stay for the learners. Even the best teachers, however, know that no one can like every student all the time.

Admittedly, some young people can be hard to like, especially students who are clearly disengaged. But as we've seen, it's not unusual for some teachers to love those kids the most. Teachers who are drawn to difficult students aren't martyrs, nor are they crazy or masochistic. Like all great teachers, they love helping people learn. And there are few greater rewards than watching a tough-to-love student start to put more effort into learning than troublemaking.

Fred, the teacher from New York, says, "I had a young boy in my class once, and according to everyone who had him before, he was a real pistol — a cute little pistol, but misguided and misdirected. Well, he was accused of a particular wrongdoing, and once you're labeled a troublemaker, you're always perceived as a troublemaker. But I gave him the benefit of the doubt, and it turned out he had nothing to do with the situation. Then everybody's attitudes about him started to change; they started giving him the benefit of the doubt. From that day on, he was only half a pistol."

Working to develop a network around the most challenging students is a common tactic used by successful teachers. They do their best to draw in family members, coaches, and other teachers — and, in some circumstances, social workers and healthcare providers — to create a world in which school becomes important and valued to the challenging students. Great teachers know that these less-than-adorable young people aren't rotten; they just have issues that conflict with their scholarship. There are few better feelings than the one teachers get when the network succeeds and the student begins to improve.

Suggesting that the networking technique always works would be the purest drivel. Sometimes the network can't be built or the student can't be drawn into it. These are the cases that prove how much teachers really care about their students because these are the cases that break teachers' hearts. As Fred says, "I say that I'll give up on a child, but I never do."

Three Things That Great Teachers Do "Wrong"

You've seen how great teachers' perceptions differ from others'; their behaviors differ too. Because these behaviors tend to run counter to what teachers learn in college and professional development seminars, they are unconventional and, simply put, unorthodox. Great teachers don't set out to be unorthodox — they don't "do wrong" for fun. They do it because there are times when doing what conventional wisdom considers the right thing is actually doing the worst thing: betraying the education of a child. One of the telltale signs of a great teacher is his or her inclination at these times to do, for the right reasons, what conventional wisdom says is wrong. Here are three examples of things great teachers do "wrong":

Create flexible structure

Though great teachers tend to be well-organized, they don't always stick to the plan. They occasionally create new lessons on the fly. And they don't treat every student the same way. "I have a boy with a learning disability, and he has a lot of trouble with spelling tests," says an eighth-grade English teacher. "One of the other boys came up to me and asked, 'Can Brian just pronounce the words and spell them for me out loud? I'll copy them down, and you can see his spelling test, because Brian does better that way.' Of course I agreed, and Brian's been doing great." Tag-team spelling was not this teacher's usual method, but the variation helped Brian.

Great teachers don't teach all their classes the same way, and they don't teach each individual class the same way every day. But they aren't chaotic. They don't make a habit of confusing students about what to do or expect. "I have structure in the sense that the students know what's going to happen throughout the period," Joanna says, "but I'll deviate and add to it. I go with the moment. I

33

don't rush through things; I go with what happens on a daily basis because you don't have the same students there every day. You have to kind of go with who's there, what we're doing, and move with it."

A great teacher has the ability to establish basic standards and develop boundaries that make it possible to deal with many students in a learning environment while adapting to the needs of those students. The inconsistency of great teachers is a product of flexibility. "I make a plan. But then I'll skip the plan. I'm adaptive," says Jane, the junior high English teacher.

Share control

Great teachers don't try to rule the classroom with an iron fist, but instead, they encourage and invite participation. They make students part of classroom management and help students assume responsibility and authority over their learning. As one teacher puts it, "I always tell them they give themselves the grades. I don't." This approach creates an atmosphere of cooperative experience, which is as powerful as it is motivating. It puts students in charge of their education, providing a powerful lesson. "A child has the right to choose to fail, though I hope no one takes me up on that option," Jane says. Quite simply, students become dependable and reliable by being given responsibility for their own learning.

Express emotions

On average, teachers spend $443 of their own money each year on classroom materials — $470 in large schools. Putting a dollar value on what is obviously emotional engagement may seem crass, but it illustrates an important point: Teachers care enough about the quality of their students' education to invest, in some cases, half a paycheck a year in materials. Great teachers know that's only one aspect of their emotional engagement.

Great teachers show their pride in and care for their students using words and actions. Our best teachers show that they are proud of their students' academic achievements and personally invested in their growth as people. Emotions are very powerful, and they transmit easily — and young people respond to them quickly. Emotion is part of being alive, so removing it deliberately restrains the art of teaching. As one teacher notes, "Teachers lose an awful lot if they don't show emotions."

Students learn more from teachers who laugh with them, cheer with them, and sometimes, cry with them. "We came in one Monday morning and found out that one of our students had been killed over the weekend," says Jackie, the teacher from Tennessee. "He had been shot in a car and just thrown out in the street to die. Of course, that's all the kids had on their minds that day. We talked about it, and I told the kids it's all right to cry. I cried. I went to the funeral home. It was a loss to me, just like it was to my students, and they needed to know that." When students see real emotion coming from a teacher, they realize that a real person is teaching them — and that teacher creates a personal, powerful presence in the classroom.

Your Turn

As mentioned at the beginning of the chapter, great teachers all share an uncanny, innate ability to reach and help people learn. That ability is an expression of talent. And that ability can be improved and leveraged in ways many teachers never realized, as you will learn in Chapter Two.

Exercise

You've read about some of the common traits and behaviors of great teachers and, no doubt, recognized some of them in other teachers or yourself. Now think about the characteristics, traits, and behaviors of the best teacher you ever had. Go ahead, write in the book. This book is yours and, literally, about you — and you'll learn a lot from this exercise when you learn more about your greatest talents and leveraging them through strengths.

1. What was the name of the best teacher you ever had?
    Ms. Bicket

2. What misinformation did that teacher reject?
    To keep professional distance. harshly rebuke

3. What "unorthodox" behavior did that teacher manifest?
    Personal interest in my life, compassionate

4. What made that teacher so memorable to you and influential on your education? Why do you still remember that teacher? *She invested into my life on a personal level. She was looking out for me & encouraged me.*

5. What did that teacher do that you've never seen another teacher attempt? *She remembered our names & really got to know us. She praised our successes.*

6. How did that teacher make you feel? *That I was 1 valuable individual in her class*

7. Do you use any of that teacher's methods, sayings, or behaviors in your own classes? *Absolutely.*

Chapter Two

Why You Are Who You Are

In the previous chapter, we probed the hearts, minds, and methods of a few of the best teachers Gallup has studied. Though it's illuminating to learn how other teachers do what they do, it's important to reiterate that, regardless of their geographical location, subject matter, experience level, and personality, those teachers all share some similarities. Later in this chapter, you'll learn why. The first thing to understand is how those shared characteristics play out in the classroom.

Starting at the Beginning

In a 1999 Gallup Poll, 89% of the American public said they favored higher pay for teachers who demonstrate top performance, and 61% favored giving them tax credits. In 2001, 54% said they would be willing to pay higher taxes if teacher pay was tied to student achievement. Clearly, people are willing to accept a higher tax burden if it means a better education for young people.

The best methods of measuring student achievement, however, are less clear. Should society use national, statewide, or local standardized tests? Non-standardized tests written by individual teachers, boards of education, outside experts? Essay tests, no tests, portfolios, criterion-referenced tests from kindergarten to 12th grade? The No Child Left Behind Act settled the question of whether testing would occur, and states now have in place some form of standards and testing for grades 3-8.

Tennessee, one of the states that first looked at statewide testing, took the next step to assess the degree to which school districts, schools, and teachers influence student achievement.

Tennessee's Assessment Model

Every spring, each third-grade through eighth-grade and high school student in Tennessee takes an achievement test that is part of the Tennessee Comprehensive Assessment Program (TCAP). The test for the younger students covers math, science, social studies, reading, and language arts. High school students must take three Gateway exams in Algebra I, Biology I, and English II. Additional end-of-year course exams are required in four core subjects.

The TCAP test results are evaluated to determine the gains made by each student and in each subject. Student gains are defined as the value added through one year of instruction. The Tennessee Value-Added Assessment System (TVAAS) uses a statistical mixed-method theory and methodology that permits it to do a multivariate, longitudinal analysis of student achievement data. In other words, they crunch a lot of numbers to create a chart of students' educational attainment during a year of instruction and over time.

Over the years, the accumulated data illustrate how much every student has learned, grade after grade, in a particular subject and for each teacher. The individual student and teacher data are confidential. But the public sees the aggregated data for school systems and individual schools across the state.

Alarming — But Effective?

Many teachers would probably find this approach alarming. Even a superior teacher can have a bad semester. Because students (and thus teachers) are evaluated every year, a bad quarter or semester or year gets folded into a running average, instead of being evaluated on its own. So TVAAS shows a student's learning arc over the course of years — a moving picture, instead of a snapshot. Of course, it shows the arc of a teacher's teaching over the course of years, too. Bad quarters are balanced by good ones — for students and teachers — and the result is a broad, averaged view of an educational career.

Nonetheless, the results are strictly tied to student performance. The worst semester of a teacher's career doesn't make up the whole picture, but there is no way to obscure that teacher's ability to teach, either. This permits researchers and Tennessee school leaders to measure the effect of a school system, schools, and teachers on student achievement. A word of caution is appropriate because the TVAAS approach is not without its critics. But the Tennessee system, with all of its limitations, does provide a glimpse into the importance of teachers.

The results of this approach have been remarkable. Students' race, gender, age, household income, class size, and cultural homogeneity don't provide an explanation of student growth in a subject from one year to the next. A highly effective teacher elicits student growth regardless of the student's background.

It gets better — and worse. TVAAS shows that the positive effects of a highly effective teacher can linger for up to three years, as can the negative effects of a highly ineffective teacher. So, a teacher's impact on student learning can be measured three years out, regardless of the effectiveness of the subsequent teachers. William Sanders, the psychologist who developed TVAAS, wrote:

> An effective teacher receiving students from a relatively ineffective teacher can facilitate excellent academic gain for his/her students during the school year. Yet these analyses suggest that the residual effects of relatively ineffective teachers from prior years can be measured in subsequent student achievement scores.

Years of TVAAS results show that the effects attributable to teachers are staggeringly important. And, "The single most dominant factor affecting student academic gain is teacher effect. . . . Groups of students with comparable abilities and initial achievement levels may have vastly different academic outcomes as a result of the sequence of teachers to which they are assigned." Sanders discovered that teacher sequence plays "a most important role" in the life opportunities of every student. In fact, it appears that the teacher is several times more important than any of the other factors, making teachers more valuable than many ever realized. (Sanders and Rivers, 1996)

Now, knowing (as a result of TVAAS) about the critical necessity of great teachers, educators are left with a few questions: What are the characteristics of great teachers? How does a school district or a principal find them? What makes them different from less effective teachers? What can we do to make every teacher a great teacher? These were the questions that inspired Gallup's years of research into teaching.

Dr. Clifton's Early Discoveries

As early as the 1950s, Dr. Donald O. Clifton, an educational psychologist at the University of Nebraska, was intrigued with the influence of teachers. Dr. Clifton — who would become Gallup's chairman, the head of Gallup University, and a driving force behind many of Gallup's studies — taught educational psychology at the University of Nebraska. One of his first assignments was to select and train freshman counselors — the professors and upperclassmen who helped freshmen develop their academic, social, leadership, and creative capacities. Some of the freshman students complained bitterly that their counseling meetings were a complete waste of time; others remarked that the sessions were the best experiences they ever had in college. Pretty quickly, Dr. Clifton figured out that all the complaining students went to the same group of counselors, and the grateful students went to another group of counselors.

Dr. Clifton took a close look at the counselors, and he realized that the ones students liked best were all alike in a remarkable way: They seemed to have similar patterns of thought, behavior, and feeling. He assembled a team of researchers and began to study the counselor issue in detail. As a result, he devised a method of counselor selection that was highly predictive of success.

That research led to other projects, including one for the campus' Naval ROTC Commandant. Dr. Clifton studied the meager 19% of students who graduated from the program and predicted which students in the next class would most likely succeed. Of those whom Dr. Clifton recommended, 78% graduated.

"The Commandant went around campus telling people he had a Ouija board," Dr. Clifton said. "As psychologists, we didn't like this at all. When you work hundreds of hours using a scientific approach, you don't like to have somebody think that it's mysterious. It was a lot of hard work."

Dr. Clifton was a popular professor at the University of Nebraska, and he had many graduate students. With his doctoral and master's degree students, he conducted numerous studies concerning human relations, positive psychology, and student-teacher rapport. He was especially interested in developing testing instruments to predict teacher performance. During the 1960s, he and his graduate students conducted a number of studies comparing Clifton-developed assessment instruments with teacher outcome measures such as student ratings of teacher effectiveness or administrator perceptions of their teachers' performance. This was original, breakthrough research that was the basis for much of Dr. Clifton's later thinking and inventions.

Eventually, Dr. Clifton left the university to start his own company, Selection Research, Inc. (SRI) — which later acquired The Gallup Organization — so that he could devote more time and resources to studying talent, how to find it, and how to deploy it. He was wildly successful — so much so that the American Psychological Association presented Dr. Clifton with a Presidential Commendation that credited him as The Father of Strengths-Based Psychology. In the last 40 years, more than two million people have been studied in dozens of industries and in hundreds of job roles — including education — in countries around the world.

In fact, research that began as the study of counselors and teachers eventually revealed some enduring truths about the way people behave on the job, no matter what job it is. This research uncovered a principle that was staggering in its implications: The differences among people influence how they do things. Each individual person has unique, innate tendencies to think, feel, and behave in certain ways most of the time. Gallup calls those prevailing thoughts, feelings, and behaviors dominant talents.

Though this sounds like common sense, this principle actually runs counter to just about everything people have been taught about themselves. What's more, this principle has altered several branches of psychology and created a new one: strengths psychology. You'll read more about this later, but strengths psychology is essentially the study of what's right with people, not what's wrong with them.

Over the years, many teachers have found strengths psychology to be quite inspiring and liberating. "It validates you. It makes life easier, and it's an extremely valuable tool," says Cathy, a high school teacher with 25 years of experience. "It teaches you to appreciate other people and the way they do things more than you did before." Another of strengths psychology's benefits is that it lays to rest a few of the more pernicious forms of educational misinformation.

Challenging Conventional Wisdom

So how does strengths psychology challenge conventional psychological wisdom? Mostly by identifying a few clear truths.

First, people tend to think that there is a continuum in roles, especially job roles. Conventional wisdom holds that there's a basic scale from 1 to 10, from ineffective teacher to effective teacher, from adequate doctor to excellent doctor. People think that totally dissimilar job roles are, well, totally dissimilar. But the truth is that there is a deep similarity among high performers in every job category. An incredibly effective teacher has more in common with an incredibly effective aeronautics engineer than with an ineffective teacher.

How? The best people, no matter what the job, are the ones who have the particular talents for the job. Great teachers, doctors, and aeronautics engineers don't behave identically at work because each of those job roles requires different responses and abilities. But great teachers, doctors, and aeronautics engineers — in effect, all exceptional workers — are nearly identical in their innate ability to function superbly in their job roles. In fact, two million interviews show that the best people in their job roles, though very different individuals, tend to answer open-ended questions with an eerie similarity.

Secondly, conventional wisdom says that studying the worst performers will show us what not to do, and by doing the opposite, we'll figure out what we ought to do. Low performers will teach us what makes high performers so successful. Nonsense. Studying low performers mostly teaches you about low performers. The truth is that studying the best is much more revealing and productive than studying the worst.

Since World War I, psychology and medicine have used a pathology model: the study of illness, what causes it, and what fixes it. You can learn a lot about illness by studying the ill, but sick people don't necessarily offer much insight into healthy people. If you want to understand the healthy, study them and how they stay that way.

Likewise, if you want to understand why ineffective teachers don't teach as well as others, study ineffective teachers. But you won't learn about great teachers that way. To understand the best, study the best. That's why Gallup has conducted so many interviews — to find the best and determine what makes them alike, not what makes them different from lesser performers. Success and failure are not opposites. Always study the best.

Third, it was thought for years that some human traits, such as empathy, competitiveness, and inquisitiveness, could not be measured. The truth is, these human traits have effects, and those effects can be measured. You can measure the immeasurable — and measurement increases success.

Say, for instance, a teacher notices that the same few students are answering all the questions, and he decides he wants all his students to participate. So, he tells the class that he expects to see more hands in the air, that he values everyone's input, and that all questions are good questions. If he stops at the installation process, his fledgling democracy will wither. He has to measure it. Of course, he can't literally measure class participation — it's too nuanced for that — but he can measure the products of participation. He can, for example, count how many students raise their hands, and he can make note of who they are. He can see how often the "leaders" step back to allow a quieter student to speak up. The more this teacher measures success, the more he can encourage and foster it.

The measurement of the immeasurable is one of the reasons TVAAS is so important. It proves, scientifically, that there are real differences among teachers. The fact that there are differences in the effectiveness of teachers has been, alas, debated. Remember the "anyone can be a teacher" myth?

So Gallup researched the best teachers in the world, didn't bother with the worst, and found ways to measure success. The most useful lesson from all those years and all that analysis is that the most harmful form of misinformation was laid to rest — the assertion that we are all the same.

The American Myth

Most people have been taught that they can do anything they set their minds to. This is particularly true in American society, where one of the predominant myths is that people can be anything they want to be if they just work hard enough. At first glance, this is inspiring and encouraging — it's at the heart of the American dream.

In reality, this myth isn't supportable, and it can actually be destructive. In the real world, if you don't have an innate talent for finding common ground among competing interests and managing people, you probably won't be an effective principal. If you don't find genuine satisfaction in organization and order, you are unlikely to have the tidiest classroom in the school. And if conflict and arguments make you uncomfortable — if you prefer harmony — you're probably not going to be an effective debate coach. Many people intuitively know this to be true. Yet they are told, from a very young age, that they can do anything, and they can be better at everything, if they just try hard enough — and try, and try, and try.

Don't bother. It's not worth it.

This appears to be a shocking statement, and it often inspires hot denials. Many people point out that practice made them good at something, which of course is true. If you practice hard, you can be better at just about anything than you were when you started. People who have practiced the piano for years are better than beginners. The twentieth speech is always better than the first.

You can't, however, be world-class at everything. In fact, you may never be more than mediocre at some things, no matter how hard you try. Why? Because you don't have the talents to be world-class at everything. On the other hand, you do have the talents to do many things very well — and some things superbly. At heart, this insight — which is the essence of strengths psychology — is far more inspiring than the "you can be anything you want" myth.

This insight has inspired Pam, an educator in Missouri. "I don't feel bad about the things I don't do well anymore," she says. "And things I used to feel bad about doing well — there are some behaviors people don't encourage — I don't feel bad about either." She adds that strengths psychology has "empowered me and helped me empower others. I'm a little more accepting of other people. I'm glad to know I'm me, and I'm okay."

Talent

Most of the time, when people speak of "talent," they're referring to the ability to do some specific — usually artistic or athletic — activity. We talk about talented singers, runners, painters, or football players. Mozart was a talented composer, and Tiger Woods is a talented golfer. That definition of talent is a bit too broad for our purposes.

Talents, as Gallup formally defines the word, are naturally recurring patterns of thought, feeling, or behavior that can be productively applied. Your talents are the ways in which you think, feel, and behave instinctively, unintentionally, and without even noticing it. You can't gain new talents by reading a book, and you won't pick them up through experience either. Your talents are the essence of your natural self. You are what you are; you aren't what you aren't.

When exceptional talents for a particular task are combined with the pertinent skills and knowledge, you have a strength — the ability to consistently perform that task at a nearly perfect level (you'll learn more about strengths later in this chapter). You might have noticed how often words like "naturally" or "instinctively" appeared in the previous chapter. It's no accident. Talents are innate; they can't be instilled, learned, or removed. But they can be identified and nurtured.

This knowledge about talent can inspire a sense of relief. "Knowing that you are what you are and knowing you have certain dominant talent themes is incredibly validating," says Marla, a veteran teacher and administration member. "I don't have to be perfect in everything. I don't have to do everything — I can't. I tell you, just knowing this stuff exists relieves a lot of stress and anxiety."

The reason we can't learn new talents or get rid of the ones we have is that talents are a manifestation of the way our brains are constructed. The fact that you have the talents to teach, but your sister doesn't, comes down to something as small as a synapse, or rather, several billion synapses. Synapses are the connections between brain cells that allow the cells to communicate with each other. That communication between brain cells is why you think, feel, and behave the way you do. That's why billions and billions of humans, who all have nearly identical physical construction, behave so differently.

Neurologists have discovered that all human brains share a similar construction pattern. Shortly after conception, 42 days in fact, the brain starts a major development project. On the 42nd day, the first brain cell, called a neuron, is formed. For another four months, 9,500 neurons form every second, 24 hours a day. By the time this growth spurt is done (at the end of the four months), the brain has accumulated billions of new brain cells. Three months later, the brain starts forming synapses in those spaces between the neurons. Each neuron reaches out for another cell — literally — with a thread-like thing called an axon. Whenever a connection is made, a synapse is formed, and the neurons keep creating synapses until long after birth. By the time a child is three, each of his billions of neurons has formed 15,000 connections. Then those connections start to disintegrate.

By the time a person is 25, all the construction work is done. The brain is pretty much complete, and half the neuron-synapse-neuron connections are gone. It's a good thing, too. Infants and toddlers are so busy soaking up stimuli in their warp-speed brains that they can't make much sense of all of it. If that continued into adulthood, we'd all be wrecks. So between the ages of 3 and 25 (though most of the work is done by the age of 15 or so), our brain begins a quality-control process, solidifying some of the connections it's made and neglecting the rest. Incidentally, if you teach adolescents, you may notice that they don't always use the best judgment. That's because the parts of the brain that control judgment aren't yet fully formed and won't be until these adolescents are in their mid-20s.

This cranial construction process can sound somewhat reductive. We have brains like the core of a nuclear reactor, but for only three years or so. Then we start losing what we so energetically built. What's the point of that? The point is that strong neural connections are really useful. Nature shuts down billions of connections so that you can focus on some and so that you don't get distracted by the ones you don't need.

Dr. Harry Chugani, a professor of pediatrics, neurology, and radiology at Wayne State University School of Medicine, offers this analogy: "Roads with the most traffic get widened. The ones that are rarely used fall into disrepair." (Coffman and Gonzalez-Molina, 2002) The connections between brain cells are a lot like roadways. The ones we use most often are broad, fast, and easy to navigate, like eight-lane interstate highways. Those are your greatest, or most dominant, talents. The connections we use less often are like city streets. Narrower and more sedate, they are noticeably slower, but they can sometimes eventually take us where we need to go. The connections we use only when we must are like gravel roads

— slow, difficult, and fraught with flaws — or even like overgrown paths in the deep woods, which we couldn't travel even if we wanted to. There really isn't much we can do about it. Nature, nurture, and experience instill and maintain those roadways from conception.

The roadways in your brain — your talents — make you who you are. And they are subtler than you may think. When you go home, do you leave your shoes at the door, put them away in your closet, or wear them until it's time to go to bed? If your spouse threw a surprise party for you, would you be delighted, anxious, or mad? Do you prefer chess or charades? These seemingly unimportant behaviors are all clues to, and exhibitions of, talents. An antique, nearly forgotten study shows how all this works in the classroom.

In the 1950s, the Nebraska School Study Council supported research into speed-reading. (Clifton and Nelson, 1992) They tested three methods — tachistoscope, film, and determined effort — on 6,000 tenth-graders across Nebraska. Which method do you think worked best? None of them. There were no statistical differences among methods in gains of words per minute. The only differences in gains of words per minute were among students. All the students who took the test made some gains. But the students who read fast at the beginning of the test were the ones who made the most gains, from 300 words per minute at the beginning of the study to 2,900 at the end, on average.

There is no speed-reading section of the human brain, so these students weren't necessarily intellectually similar. What they brought to the study that the slower readers didn't was a variety of talents that helped them learn how to read fast. This is also likely to be the reason they were fast readers before they were trained to be by these methods. The students who made only minimal gains, from 90 words per minute to 150 at the end, probably didn't have the talents to learn how to read fast, so they didn't get much out of the lesson — and never would, no matter how much they tried.

Weaknesses

The idea that people should work very hard to do things they aren't naturally good at for the sake of being well-rounded is a mistake. Everyone already has a unique set of talents that are tremendously powerful and the potential basis for strengths. When you're busily trying to fix a lesser talent — a weakness — you're ignoring your far more effective talents, perhaps even ignoring some fully developed strengths.

Sadly, people are usually more familiar with their weaknesses than with their strengths and dominant talents. Because weaknesses are perceived as problem areas, because they can be embarrassing, and because others might point them out, people tend to know their weaknesses well. And because the pathology method isn't limited to the field of psychology but is standard practice in just about every field, including education, most people spend an awful lot of time trying to fix their weaknesses.

Ultimately, however, fixing weaknesses is impossible. Weaknesses are your brain's rough roads and overgrown paths, and trying to make them useful usually isn't worth the effort, especially when an eight-lane superhighway is a few neurons away. Working on weaknesses means that you keep doing, with dogged and pained determination, what you don't — and can't — do well. Even with all that effort, the best you can hope to become is mediocre.

Just ask Jennifer, an education writer. "I was never very good at math, though all my other grades were fine," she says. "I was in remedial math and the gifted student program at the same time. By sixth grade, I had a weekly math tutor. In junior high, I was taking the math textbook home every summer and redoing what I'd done all year. It only got worse in college. I flunked all my university's math classes. In the end, I took a syllogistic logic class because it was the only class I hadn't yet flunked that fit the requirement — and I got an A+."

It wasn't until Jennifer learned more about some of her top talent themes — Analytical, Achiever, Focus, and Ideation — that she figured out why she got an A in a tough math class. "All those years, I was trying to learn math by rote memorization, which I'm bad at, instead of using logical thinking, which I'm great at — it's one of my most dominant talents," Jennifer says. "But I'm mad that I spent so much time trying to fix my math problem when I could have focused my attention on things that I naturally do well."

In a way, your weaknesses are like your greatest talents: They're innate, and you can't get rid of them. The best thing to do is manage them or work around them. We tend to forget that other people can help us manage our weaknesses because we assume that everybody has the same ones we do. Because we are so familiar with them, because they're set so deep in our brains, because they're so close, we tend to think our weaknesses are universal. They aren't — your weakness may be someone else's dominant talent.

"If an activity takes too long, I lose interest," says a teacher whose most dominant talent theme is Activator. "So, to work around that, I'll tell people that I'm feeling unmotivated and ask for help. Just knowing that someone is making a special trip to help me makes me rush around and get things done."

There are many ways to reduce or eliminate the negative effects of the lesser talents referred to as weaknesses. Here are some ideas to get you started:

- Find a partner. If, for example, you have little talent for organization, but you need it to do your job, seek out someone who's naturally more organized. Or if you are not at all creative but need art ideas for your class, ask a creative colleague for thoughts. Offer your talents in return. You and your partner will both be more effective and more productive.

- If your weakness is a deficiency in skill or knowledge, a little effort will rectify it. For example, if your weakness is punctuation and you teach language, brush up on the rules — just like you expect your students to do. Learn what you need to learn, and practice what you need to practice.

- If the weakness doesn't relate to skills or knowledge, but it concerns something you *have* to do, something you can't ignore, the only thing to do is get a little better at it. If, for instance, your talents in communication are very weak, but you have to communicate with your peers, your only option is to hunker down and work on it. This is exactly what you tell your students when they're faced with something they're not good at and don't want to do. You'll never achieve excellence, but you should be able to improve modestly.

- Weakness management systems are tremendously useful. One teacher Gallup interviewed had such a chronically short attention span that she could not stay focused long enough to grade all her students' papers. She dealt with it by developing a management system: She never marked more than five papers at a time. Once five were done, she got up and fed the cat. Another five, then she got a cup of coffee. The system took her weakness into account and worked around it.

Strengths

Talents, in Gallup's definition, aren't necessarily abilities to perform particular activities like golf or musical composition. They are a deeply ingrained aspect of one's psychology and personality — and they are permanent. But talents are not strengths. The strengths of great teachers are based on talent, but they also contain one part skill and one part knowledge. It's only when talent, knowledge, and skill are combined that they become a strength.

If talent is an innate way of thinking, feeling, or behaving, what are knowledge and skill? Knowledge is the stuff you know — facts you have learned, such as the chemical compound of gunpowder, who wrote *Jane Eyre*, or how to calculate square roots. Unlike talents, you can always obtain more knowledge. Very few professions are as well-situated to the accumulation of knowledge as teaching, and many teachers have a talent for gaining knowledge.

A skill is the ability to perform the basic steps of an activity, such as operating a computer keyboard, performing the basic motions of throwing a ball, or using a particular software to carry out the fundamental steps of creating a presentation. Skills improve with repeated use and can be taught, but you can't always obtain them. If you pick up a new activity and find your skill in it is nearly perfect from the very start, you probably have the necessary talents for it, like those successful speed-readers in Nebraska. On the other hand, if a skill doesn't come to you quickly and easily, your most dominant talents probably lie in another area.

So talent is an innate ability, knowledge is factual information and awareness gained through experience, and skill is the ability to perform the basic steps of an activity. A strength is a combination of natural ability, education, and training that produces consistent, near-perfect performance in a specific task. Strengths are what make great teachers great.

In fact, the underlying similarity of all great teachers is that they capitalize on their teaching talents and develop strengths. Strengths are powerful, and the more you use them, the more powerful they become — just like a muscle in your body. When you teach with talent, knowledge, and skill — when you teach with your strengths — you have what you need to be a remarkably effective educator.

That's one of the most valuable findings from decades of data from the TVAAS. Year after year, men and women who teach with strengths, even if they are completely unaware that that's what they are doing, are turning out well-educated students. Those students, regardless of their socioeconomic status, go on to be good students. And, unless they get stuck with an untalented teacher, those young people in Tennessee leave school with all the best a great teacher can give them.

By now, you would probably like to get on with it and learn about your top themes of talent and get some suggestions on how to develop strengths. We'll cover that in the following chapters.

Chapter Three

Discovering Your Signature Themes

On the first day of each school year, every student is a stranger. You don't know how these young people will learn, what they're good at, how they'll respond to you — each one is a mystery. But after a while, you discover your students' personalities from what they do, what they say, and how they say it. Each student becomes distinct because you pick up on his or her personal characteristics.

The Clifton StrengthsFinder assessment, which you will take, does the same sort of thing — but faster and supported by decades of research. Your responses to the assessment reveal your own unique psychological makeup. The Clifton StrengthsFinder is designed to elicit, sort, and score key indications of your personality based on the responses you give to it. Designed by Dr. Donald O. Clifton, along with leading psychologists, linguists, survey experts, and content analysts, the assessment helps you uncover your most dominant talents (your innate patterns of thought, feeling, and behavior that can be productively applied) in 34 important areas (themes).

There are no right or wrong answers, of course, and the Clifton StrengthsFinder is designed to prevent you from over-thinking your responses; you only have 20 seconds to read and respond, so your answers are top-of-mind. You'll immediately receive your top five, or Signature, talent themes upon completion. All Clifton StrengthsFinder reports are completely confidential. However, you're encouraged to share your themes, especially with colleagues. Helping people get a better sense of your talents will permit them to work more effectively with you. Your friends and family can be great resources, too.

Don't be surprised if the results are uncannily personal and accurate. One woman who took the assessment says, "It was eerie. It told me things about myself that I didn't think anyone knew. I've been trying to downplay my competitiveness for years, but Competition was among my top five themes."

Your Clifton StrengthsFinder report is only a starting point. To make your talents powerful in the classroom, you'll have to augment them with skills and knowledge to build strengths. You were born with talents, but strengths are earned.

Before taking the assessment, review the following strengths terminology:

Your **talents** are the ways in which you naturally think, feel, and behave. The inner drive to compete, sensitivity to the needs of others, and the tendency to be socially outgoing are examples of talents. Talents exist naturally; they cannot be acquired.

Your **greatest, or dominant, talents** are the ways in which you most naturally think, feel, or behave. For that reason, they afford the best opportunity for excellence.

The Clifton StrengthsFinder measures your talents in 34 areas, or **themes**. Each of these areas contains innumerable talents. The Clifton StrengthsFinder provides a clue to your greatest talents by revealing the five areas in which they are likely to be found.

Yearnings, rapid learning, satisfactions, and **timelessness** are other clues to your greatest talents.

- **Yearnings** reveal the presence of a talent, particularly when they are felt early in life. A yearning can be described as a pull or a magnetic influence that draws you to a particular activity or environment time and again.

- **Rapid learning** offers another trace of talent. In the context of a new challenge or a new environment, something sparks your talent. Immediately, your brain seems to light up as if a whole bank of switches were suddenly flicked to "on." The speed at which you learn a new skill or gain new knowledge provides a telltale clue to the talent's presence and power.

- **Satisfactions** are psychological fulfillments that result when you take on and successfully meet "challenges" that engage your greatest talents. Pay close attention to the situations that seem to bring you these energizing satisfactions. If you can identify them, you are well on your way to pinpointing your talents.

- **Timelessness** can also serve as a clue to talent. If you have ever become so engrossed in an activity that you lost all track of time, it may have been because the activity engaged you at a deep, natural level — the level of talent.

A **strength** is the ability to consistently provide near-perfect performance in a specific task — for instance, lesson planning or coaching basketball. A strength is the desired outcome of strengths development, and it is usually composed of talents, skills, and knowledge. It always begins with the right talents for the task.

A **skill** is the basic ability to perform the steps of specific tasks, such as the ability to type. Skills do not naturally exist within us, but they can be acquired through training.

Knowledge is what you know. Knowledge includes the hard facts you have grasped and understanding that you have gained through experience. Knowledge does not naturally exist within us, but it can be acquired through education.

Your **weaknesses** are your areas of lesser skill, knowledge, or talent. They are a concern only when they can negatively affect outcomes. Then, they should be managed. Weaknesses in skill can often be managed through training. Weaknesses in knowledge can be managed through education. Weaknesses in talent can be managed through support systems and complementary partnerships.

A **support system** is a tool that compensates for a weakness — a lack of talent, skill, and/or knowledge. A support system may be as simple as a calculator for a person with a weakness in math, or a to-do list for a person who has difficulty maintaining focus or feeling a sense of achievement.

A **complementary partnership** exists when you compensate for a weakness by partnering with a person who is particularly talented, skilled, and/or knowledgeable in the area of your weakness.

How to Take the Clifton StrengthsFinder

The Clifton StrengthsFinder is a 30-minute, Web-based assessment that measures the presence of talent in 34 themes. Immediately after you complete your assessment, you will receive a report of your Signature Themes — your top five themes of talent — as indicated by your responses.

We encourage you to get the most out of your Clifton Strengths-Finder report by keeping these things in mind:

- Remember that the purpose of the Clifton StrengthsFinder process is to strengthen your awareness of your own innate talents and how you can use those talents more intentionally in the future. Often, our talents seem ordinary to us because they come so naturally to us.

- Read each theme description, and highlight the phrases or sentences that you believe really fit you. Cross out phrases that don't seem to apply to you. Tailor each Signature Theme description to match your talents.

- Write down a recent situation or instance in which you have put each Signature Theme into action.

- Ask family, friends, and colleagues to respond to and affirm your Signature Themes.

It's time. You are ready to begin. This is your chance to learn your Signature Themes through your own Clifton StrengthsFinder assessment. To begin, find the ID code that is located on the reverse side of the jacket of this book. Then go to www.strengthsfinder.com. Please note that each ID code provides only one Clifton Strengths-Finder assessment.

The minimum system requirements for the Clifton Strengths-Finder Web site are:

- 33.6K modem (56K modem or faster recommended)

- Internet Explorer 5.0 or Netscape Navigator 4.03

Chapter Four

Putting Your Talents to Work

T aking the Clifton StrengthsFinder assessment can be a lot of fun, and seeing the results is exciting. But discovering your top five themes is only a starting point. Though the themes provide tremendous insight into your natural potential, you must take action if you are to maximize that potential.

As noted earlier, you're born with talents, but strengths are earned. You have to add knowledge and skill to your talents to build strengths. An important step in creating a teaching strength is figuring out how to leverage your talents — and do it in a way that's specific to the teaching profession. That's difficult to do without some coaching.

In this chapter, you'll find, in alphabetical order, descriptions of each of the 34 themes of talent measured by the Clifton Strengths-Finder. Each theme description is accompanied by several "action items" — ideas for developing and deploying your talents in ways that are particular to the nature of that theme and specific to teaching. For each theme, we also offer quotes from real teachers — quotes drawn from the thousands of interviews that Gallup has conducted with educators around the world.

So look up your top themes of talent. Read what Gallup scientists and real-life teachers know about the talents they have and how to use them. Consider ways to leverage your talents in your school. Make some plans that will produce tangible strengths-development results.

Knowing your top themes is only the first step in a journey. You're halfway there when you discover the talents those themes hold and how you can build on them to create strengths.

Achiever

Your Achiever theme helps explain your drive. Achiever describes a constant need for achievement. You feel as if every day starts at zero. By the end of the day you must achieve something tangible in order to feel good about yourself. And by "every day" you mean every single day — workdays, weekends, vacations. No matter how much you may feel you deserve a day of rest, if the day passes without some form of achievement, no matter how small, you will feel dissatisfied. You have an internal fire burning inside you. It pushes you to do more, to achieve more. After each accomplishment is reached, the fire dwindles for a moment, but very soon it rekindles itself, forcing you toward the next accomplishment. Your relentless need for achievement might not be logical. It might not even be focused. But it will always be with you. As an Achiever you must learn to live with this whisper of discontent. It does have its benefits. It brings you the energy you need to work long hours without burning out. It is the jolt you can always count on to get you started on new tasks, new challenges. It is the power supply that causes you to set the pace and define the levels of productivity for your work group. It is the theme that keeps you moving.

Achiever action items:

- Your natural determination and diligence are probably key factors in your success as an educator, as you consistently commit long hours to the hard work of teaching. Because people know that you will do whatever it takes to finish any project you begin, your services are in great demand. Even though you have more energy and stamina than most, give thought to how you can maximize your time and energy.

Consider limiting your commitments to those that provide the biggest return on your investment. That will help ensure that your efforts are always aligned with your ultimate goals.

- Motivation is seldom a problem for you. A consummate self-starter, you have an internal drive toward completion that needs little external support or stimulation. The potency of your own internal drive could make it difficult for you to understand and appreciate those who are more externally motivated. Explore and identify unique and multiple sources of motivation and how they might provide the drive that is desperately needed by an under-performing student.

- Progress and improvement are likely to be prominent among your values. When you reach a particular level of achievement, you automatically ask, "What's the next level?" While this is your default setting, don't automatically assume that others will be ready for the next step as quickly as you are. In fact, some might be content with their present status and simply want to solidify and enrich that status quo. Before you push a student to the next level of some educational enterprise, be sure your need to achieve is matched by a comparable need, desire, or potential in the student. It may be possible to push a student to an educational altitude that is beyond his or her capacity to thrive.

- The pace of your life and work is likely to be faster than that of others. Just like an athlete who needs to reach a target heart rate to receive the maximum physical benefits of exercise, you simply feel better emotionally when you are operating at high levels of intensity and speed. Intentionally schedule "breaks" during which you fully relax or are at least committed to a more leisurely pace. You probably don't need the rest, but when you give those who have a hard time matching your intensity and speed an opportunity to connect with you at their own pace, they will be much more likely to stay with you as you get back to full speed.

- Your pause button is probably not very prominent. The completion of a task or an assignment brings you an immediate and corresponding sense of satisfaction and reward. Rather than pausing to thoroughly enjoy that moment, you instinctively move on to the next item on your to-do list. Consider becoming more familiar with your pause button. Before you jump into what's next, take a bit longer to study and celebrate your success. Such a pause could lead to even greater productivity and progress as you gain insights that can help you work smarter and address the motivational needs of others on your team.

Achiever in teachers sounds like this:

"I can't just do a little of something, which is why my principal gives me projects. She knows I'll work at it until the project's done, no matter what."

"Achievers are the volunteers, the committee members. When people are looking for someone to do stuff, I know I may as well raise my hand at the beginning because I know I'll wind up doing it."

Activator

"When can we start?" This is a recurring question in your life. You are impatient for action. You may concede that analysis has its uses or that debate and discussion can occasionally yield some valuable insights, but deep down you know that only action is real. Only action can make things happen. Only action leads to performance. Once a decision is made, you can't *not* act. Others may worry that "there are still some things we don't know," but this doesn't seem to slow you. If the decision has been made to go across town, you know that the fastest way to get there is to go stoplight to stoplight. You are not going to sit around waiting until all the lights have turned green. Besides, in your view, action and thinking are not opposites. In fact, guided by your Activator theme, you believe that action is the best device for learning. You make a decision, you take action, you look at the result, and you learn. This learning informs your next action and your next. How can you grow if you have nothing to react to? Well, you believe you can't. You must put yourself out there. You must take the next step. It is the only way to keep your thinking fresh and informed. The bottom line is this: You know you will be judged not by what you say, not by what you think, but by what you get done. This does not frighten you. It pleases you.

Activator action items:

- Naturally influential, you probably excel at getting people moving. Although some may be a bit intimidated by your "let's do it now" approach, many are inspired by your commitment to action. Educational projects or programs that are characterized by lethargy and inertia might drive you crazy, but consider them opportunities for your talents. Diplomatically use your catalytic push to create some much-needed momentum in these areas.

- You may have cognitively and creatively gifted students in your classroom. Their minds are filled with innovative dreams and revolutionary thoughts that could have a tremendously beneficial impact. Identify a couple of students whose dreams and theories seem to hold the most promise, and partner with them. Who knows what might happen when you help a student transform his or her brilliant conceptual theories into basic concrete action?

- Every school espouses a certain set of educational values and beliefs. They are often displayed artistically or discussed religiously. From your perspective, that isn't enough. You know that educational values "talk" is never a substitute for educational values "walk." Be an activist who regularly identifies important educational beliefs and seeks to transform them into immediate educational behavior. You will help shrink the gap that often exists between ideals and what is made real. You'll also satisfy your psychological craving for action while improving your school.

- Getting started is difficult for many people. Some remain at the starting lines of life because they feel they can proceed only "when everything is right." Help your students and colleagues know that fast starts are not necessarily an enemy of quality outcomes. Remind them that by taking action as soon as possible, they can ensure tangible results — and that by following their talents, they will naturally ensure quality by sticking to it until "everything is right."

- It's possible that you don't particularly enjoy involvement in planning teams or educational committees because from your perspective, they are more about discussion than they are about action. However, your participation may be critical to their success. Volunteer to join a team with values and goals that match your own. From the start, make it clear that you hope to help team members by moving them to action. You may not be particularly equipped for the discussion and debate that often precedes most decisions, but you are likely to be very well-suited for the action phase that must follow each decision.

Activator in teachers sounds like this:

"I'm always on the lookout for new projects that will inspire my students to take some form of action. Get the students moving, and you'll have them learning, too."

"I like to ask students to join together to make good things happen in their learning experiences. I did this a lot as a music teacher: I made music programs happen through the students' efforts, and those programs resulted in the students really feeling like they did something significant."

Adaptability

You live in the moment. You don't see the future as a fixed destination. Instead, you see it as a place that you create out of the choices that you make right now. And so you discover your future one choice at a time. This doesn't mean that you don't have plans. You probably do. But this theme of Adaptability does enable you to respond willingly to the demands of the moment even if they pull you away from your plans. Unlike some, you don't resent sudden requests or unforeseen detours. You expect them. They are inevitable. Indeed, on some level you actually look forward to them. You are, at heart, a very flexible person who can stay productive when the demands of work are pulling you in many different directions at once.

Adaptability action items:

- Change probably doesn't frighten you. In fact, you tend to respond to rapid and frequent change with flexibility and ease. Your Adaptability talents may equip you for the most spontaneous and ambiguous educational environments. Your school or district is likely to have situations and students that force teachers to think on their feet and roll with the punches. These situations and students present you with an opportunity to flex your Adaptability muscles. Gravitate toward them. Your ability to effectively cope with change and all of its implications could help create a classroom or school culture that embraces and fosters continual change. Isn't that what learning and growing is ultimately about?

- Don't let your goals become too future-oriented. You might have a tendency to procrastinate if your goals become too far removed from your present reality. You are likely to be most motivated as a teacher when you can see concrete impact in the present rather than possible impact in the future. If you are responsible for your students' long-term educational goals, break them down into daily or weekly increments.

- You will often bring emotional stability to the educational environments you inhabit. While some educators might become frazzled and frustrated by the uncontrollable factors that arise in the classroom, you will often see such intrusions as wonderful teaching moments that encourage students to make new discoveries about themselves and their world. Find ways to capture and measure the quantity and quality of these naturally occurring teaching moments so you can become even more astute and discerning about discoveries that arise from the curriculum of life.

- Highly aware of "the here and now," you probably have a keen understanding of the reality and culture of your educational institution. Be sure to share your unique perspective with school leaders. Their understanding can be clouded by their distance from the educational front line of the classroom, and they might be oriented more toward the past or the future than the present. Your real-time, real-world perspective will provide a baseline of what *is* as your school plans and works for what *could be*.

- Because of your Adaptability talents, you are more prepared than most to accept and deal with difficulties and stressful moments. Use your exceptional ability to help students debrief immediately after difficult experiences such as classroom conflicts, illness or death, or even issues of national or worldwide impact. With your assistance, students will get through — and possibly even benefit from — issues that might typically have been too much for them.

Adaptability in teachers sounds like this:

"My principal called me during the summer last year to tell me she was moving me to a different classroom, and she seemed really surprised when I didn't have a problem with it. I love change. Without it, every year is the same."

"Some of my best ideas for the classroom come to me while I'm teaching, right as I'm up there at the board. If I'm tied to a schedule or calendar, I won't be able to implement them."

Analytical

Your Analytical theme challenges other people: "Prove it. Show me why what you are claiming is true." In the face of this kind of questioning some will find that their brilliant theories wither and die. For you, this is precisely the point. You do not necessarily want to destroy other people's ideas, but you do insist that their theories be sound. You see yourself as objective and dispassionate. You like data because they are value free. They have no agenda. Armed with these data, you search for patterns and connections. You want to understand how certain patterns affect one another. How do they combine? What is their outcome? Does this outcome fit with the theory being offered or the situation being confronted? These are your questions. You peel the layers back until, gradually, the root cause or causes are revealed. Others see you as logical and rigor-ous. Over time they will come to you in order to expose someone's "wishful thinking" or "clumsy thinking" to your refining mind. It is hoped that your analysis is never delivered too harshly. Otherwise, others may avoid you when that "wishful thinking" is their own.

Analytical action items:

- You don't tend to accept new teaching theories or programs at face value; you might even find yourself in heated debates until you're convinced that the research is good. Don't expect everyone to know how important this is to you or what the standard should be. Tell your colleagues what you're looking for. Make sure that those around you understand that your skepticism is about the data, not the people behind the data — you can avoid a lot of hurt feelings that way.

- Cause and effect is more obvious to you than it is to other people. You can identify the actions that precipitate events or effects without really thinking about it. So when a student is confused or surprised by something, you can help by showing him or her the causal relationships. This can be very helpful, especially to young people, because it provides a deeper understanding and appreciation of reality.

- Your students will often find themselves in emotionally charged situations, and occasionally, your colleagues will too. You, however, are uniquely equipped to see the logic of life. When emotions are running high, consider being the voice of reason.

- Your way of dealing with complexity is to dissect it. By nature, you tend to disassemble complex concepts, view each one closely, and figure out how they work together — or what went wrong. This can be tremendously useful to others, so pay attention to how you do it. Analyze the steps that you naturally take when you break ideas down to their component parts. Don't forget to explain this process to others so they can see how you reach your conclusions. Because this comes naturally to you, the process is nearly instantaneous. Other people may not understand or even see how you do what you do.

- As an analytical person, you'll find that you're intrigued by, maybe even compelled to understand, what's going on around you and why it's happening. You grasp the logic of situations when other people miss it. This can help you help others understand their lives, though it's wise to be tactful when offering what you can so plainly see. People who depend on their own emotional feedback might consider your clear-eyed evaluation chilly.

- Because of your Analytical talents, people might see you as a serious person. There's nothing wrong with that, and there's a lot that's right. This talent can be highly effective in the classroom and even more so when you're working with your administration. It's a good idea to get some feedback from other teachers and your students about how your Analytical talent contributes to your teaching — and how it can detract. Seriousness can get a lot of work done, but it can be confused with coldness.

Analytical in teachers sounds like this:

"I'm always surprised that more people can't see the consequences of their actions and that they can't figure out how they got where they are. It always seems so obvious to me."

"I like to figure out where each student is in the learning process, what he or she will need in that process, and what I should expect along the way, of course."

Arranger

You are a conductor. When faced with a complex situation involving many factors, you enjoy managing all of the variables, aligning and realigning them until you are sure you have arranged them in the most productive configuration possible. In your mind there is nothing special about what you are doing. You are simply trying to figure out the best way to get things done. But others, lacking this theme, will be in awe of your ability. "How can you keep so many things in your head at once?" they will ask. "How can you stay so flexible, so willing to shelve well-laid plans in favor of some brand-new configuration that has just occurred to you?" But you cannot imagine behaving in any other way. You are a shining example of effective flexibility, whether you are changing travel schedules at the last minute because a better fare has popped up or mulling over just the right combination of people and resources to accomplish a new project. From the mundane to the complex, you are always looking for the perfect configuration. Of course, you are at your best in dynamic situations. Confronted with the unexpected, some complain that plans devised with such care cannot be changed, while others take refuge in the existing rules or procedures. You don't do either. Instead, you jump into the confusion, devising new options, hunting for new paths of least resistance, and figuring out new partnerships — because, after all, there might just be a better way.

Arranger action items:

- You naturally understand that effective education is the result of the complex interaction of students, curriculum, and the learning environment. In your mind, the chemistry of this interaction is seldom a fixed formula, so you continuously fine-tune and tweak it, always looking for a better way to help students learn. While your approach is quite instinctive, be intentional about explaining your rationale for such changes so others can be aware of the changes and the potential benefits.

- Because of your Arranger talents, human puzzles are easy for you to put together. Get involved in decisions about the partnering of teachers, students, or parents in your classroom, school, or district. The groups you create will often be efficient and effective in their collaboration, so offer your help in completing the education picture.

- Many of the most important accomplishments in life require cooperation and collaboration, and talented Arrangers like you are often exceptional contributors in that environment. In fact, you are likely to be much happier and more productive as an involved team member than as an individual. How many educational teams, groups, or committees are you involved in? Consider whether you can increase that number by one or two. It will keep you "in the zone" and will make your Arranger talent more productive.

- Some people tend to observe; others tend to participate. Think about instances in which your Arranger talents may have naturally led you to convert observers into participants. How did you do it? What key factors led to your success in motivating people to become involved and take action? When you isolate those factors, look for more opportunities to leverage them with students, parents, and other teachers who are prime candidates for engagement and growth.

- Flexibility is in your DNA. For you, nothing is etched in stone. You are open to consider changes that have the potential to improve performance. Let your flexibility assist you when confronted with a student who has fallen into an unsuccessful and unproductive rut. Trust and rely on your willingness and openness to adjust the educational process to achieve improved student outcomes. Be creative and flexible in your persistence.

Arranger in teachers sounds like this:

"Have you ever noticed how some people or groups just work really well together and others don't? I can always tell when it's not going to work and when it's going to work well."

"I like to create study groups. In a good study group with the right mix of students, the students can bounce their thoughts off each other, and they get more out of the lesson."

Belief

If you possess a strong Belief theme, you have certain core values that are enduring. These values vary from one person to another, but ordinarily your Belief theme causes you to be family-oriented, altruistic, even spiritual, and to value responsibility and high ethics — both in yourself and others. These core values affect your behavior in many ways. They give your life meaning and satisfaction; in your view, success is more than money and prestige. They provide you with direction, guiding you through the temptations and distractions of life toward a consistent set of priorities. This consistency is the foundation for all your relationships. Your friends call you dependable. "I know where you stand," they say. Your Belief makes you easy to trust. It also demands that you find work that meshes with your values. Your work must be meaningful; it must matter to you. And guided by your Belief theme it will matter only if it gives you a chance to live out your values.

Belief action items:

- Is your enthusiasm flagging? Is your energy waning? It could be that you are paying too much attention to the "what" and "how" of your work and not enough to the "why." People with dominant Belief talents need the "why." Go back to the exercise in Chapter One and see what you wrote about the teacher who made the most difference in your life. Recall the contributions he or she made to your growth and direction. Use this teacher's models as a source of daily inspiration as you pour your life into your students. Also, spend time with peers and colleagues who share your sense of mission.

Your time together will sharpen and intensify beliefs and increase your impact for the cause.

- You are likely to be a values-driven person. In fact, some of your values are so solid and permanent that you might even be willing to die for them. Continue to develop greater clarity in regard to these stable values so that you are able to communicate their essence. When people know what you stand for, they will more easily understand, relate to, and support your educational efforts.

- We live in a world that is characterized by rapid and extensive change. Some of the students you teach will experience anxiety and fear as they face an uncertain and unpredictable future. Make your students aware of the unchangeable values that they can always count on in your classroom. The stability of the environment you provide will lead to a sense of safety and greater productivity.

- As a belief-driven person, you may have little patience for unethical behavior. When a student violates one of your ethical standards, it will usually bring about a swift and strong response. Make sure that your students understand what you will and will not tolerate and the consequences of accepting or rejecting those standards. In addition, don't try to prevent unethical behavior through punishment alone. Come up with a proactive strategy to promote ethical behavior by recognizing and rewarding it.

- Like anyone else, you care about issues that affect your own life. Your greatest motivation, however, will often come when you get involved in issues that push you beyond the borders of your own life and force you to sacrifice something for the sake of a greater good. Identify a sacrifice you could make to contribute to a greater good in the life of a student or an educational program, and bring your beliefs to life.

Belief in teachers sounds like this:

"My belief in education is why I'm here. My belief that young people can learn and succeed is why I keep going."

"I believe that education is important. That's why I come down so hard on students who don't follow the rules. Cheating is not only wrong; it prevents the student from receiving an education."

Command

Command leads you to take charge. Unlike some people, you feel no discomfort with imposing your views on others. On the contrary, once your opinion is formed, you need to share it with others. Once your goal is set, you feel restless until you have aligned others with you. You are not frightened by confrontation; rather, you know that confrontation is the first step toward resolution. Whereas others may avoid facing up to life's unpleasantness, you feel compelled to present the facts or the truth, no matter how unpleasant it may be. You need things to be clear between people and challenge them to be clear-eyed and honest. You push them to take risks. You may even intimidate them. And while some may resent this, labeling you opinionated, they often willingly hand you the reins. People are drawn toward those who take a stance and ask them to move in a certain direction. Therefore, people will be drawn to you. You have presence. You have Command.

Command action items:

- You tend to voice thoughts that your peers and partners might not dare to express. You know that this direct approach can be much more effective than a more passive attitude. Let your peers and students know that you can be a powerful and articulate advocate on their behalf when they are hesitant to express their thoughts and feelings. While this risky and bold approach may frighten and intimidate some, it will also illuminate what others are really thinking and feeling, and it will initiate important communication and changes.

- Crisis and conflict paralyze some people, but that kind of turbulence may bring out the best in you. You are comfortable with taking charge and making difficult decisions, and that will often cause others to look to you when times are tough. Become aware of the challenging or pressure-packed situations in your classroom or school, and get yourself in a position to provide much-needed leadership through your powerful presence and personality.

- Because of your personal power, you will often be able to keep students moving forward by helping them get what they need to be successful. You will not shrink from asking for what students need, nor from applying pressure to move barriers to student success. To increase the benefit of your natural ability, measure the number of requests you make and the number of barriers you remove on behalf of your students or colleagues each week. Then seek to increase those requests and removals by one each week. This advocacy will pave the way for more productive educational environments.

- Your love of challenges often propels you out of comfort zones and into new and uncharted territory. Consider the possibility that others who are less bold might benefit from the same experience. When you decide to go on a challenging adventure, take along a passenger or two who would benefit from the experience and probably never do it on their own. Your students will experience growth opportunities just by being your passenger.

- Your naturally decisive personality will often capture the interest and respect of students, fellow teachers, and administrators in need of the clarity you can provide. Consider volunteering to take charge of a polarized or conflicted group of students, teachers, or administrators. Decisions will be made, and action will be taken. This will be tremendously satisfying to your Command talent.

Command in teachers sounds like this:

"I have no problem stating my expectations of the students, and I'm always ready to serve as an advocate for students."

"I can easily take charge of classrooms that may seem difficult to others."

Communication

You like to explain, to describe, to host, to speak in public, and to write. This is your Communication theme at work. Ideas are a dry beginning. Events are static. You feel a need to bring them to life, to energize them, to make them exciting and vivid. And so you turn events into stories and practice telling them. You take the dry idea and enliven it with images and examples and metaphors. You believe that most people have a very short attention span. They are bombarded by information, but very little of it survives. You want your information — whether an idea, an event, a product's features and benefits, a discovery, or a lesson — to survive. You want to divert their attention toward you and then capture it, lock it in. This is what drives your hunt for the perfect phrase. This is what draws you toward dramatic words and powerful word combinations. This is why people like to listen to you. Your word pictures pique their interest, sharpen their world, and inspire them to act.

Communication action items:

- Silence is not necessarily golden for you — in fact, you might find it uncomfortable. You probably place a high value on human interaction. Words, and the way they are used, are very important to you. Words are the critical currency you use in your teaching every day. Pay close attention to the words you use. Expand your vocabulary, but always match your communication to your audience. Deliberately create a classroom culture that is characterized by dialogue — it will be a learning environment that maximizes your Communication talents.

- This cluster of talents may have equipped you to be an exceptional conversationalist. You don't just talk to people; you talk with people — and this is enormously valuable in the classroom. The more you keep the conversation going, the more your students will benefit, and the stronger this talent will become. Keep track of the number of one-on-one conversations you have with your students in a week, and use it as a baseline measurement. Think about who might benefit from a talk with you. Find a way to increase the number of individual interactions a little each week — you might be surprised at how much better you function as a teacher and how much more your students learn. Don't discount the value of this talent in dealing with your colleagues. An aptly timed chat can do a world of good, and you're uniquely talented to find the words.

- You, more so than other people, are highly aware of the correlation between entertainment and education. You instinctively understand that a bored student is probably not growing or learning or achieving. You'll also be naturally attuned to signs of boredom in your classroom — keep an arsenal of methods at hand to combat it. You'll feel better, and so will your students.

- It will be the rare student who is as articulate as you are. Enjoy that student, but use your Communication talents to help everybody else put their thoughts and feelings into words. Sometimes, that's the first step toward real learning. For most young people, concepts make more sense when they are put into their own words — and you're uniquely capable of figuring out those words. Your grasp of and love for language can make you a valuable translator.

- You might find that storytelling comes to you very naturally. Collect your favorite stories, and practice telling them. You'll discover the most entertaining nuances, and knowing them will help you tell the story. Pay attention to the effect of your stories on your students. No matter what you teach, be sure to weave stories into the curriculum. The eyes may be windows to the soul, but stories are the highways to understanding.

Communication in teachers sounds like this:

"I tell stories that bring drama to the classroom. That makes people listen and learn."

"In an eighth-grade class, we were talking about perception — how five people who observe the same accident will each report it in a different way. I partnered with a student in a great experiment: We agreed that he would be late to class the next day, and I'd get all over him, which was very unlike me, and he'd yell and scream, which was totally out of character for him. We carried out our plan the next day, and we got the reaction we expected. The students were surprised and confused. Then we let them in on it, and I asked them to write about the experience. Their reactions — from their many perspectives — were really interesting, and through the discussion that followed, the students learned a lot about individual perception."

Competition

Competition is rooted in comparison. When you look at the world, you are instinctively aware of other people's performance. Their performance is the ultimate yardstick. No matter how hard you tried, no matter how worthy your intentions, if you reached your goal but did not outperform your peers, the achievement feels hollow. Like all competitors, you need other people. You need to compare. If you can compare, you can compete, and if you can compete, you can win. And when you win, there is no feeling quite like it. You like measurement because it facilitates comparisons. You like other competitors because they invigorate you. You like contests because they must produce a winner. You particularly like contests where you know you have the inside track to be the winner. Although you are gracious to your fellow competitors and even stoic in defeat, you don't compete for the fun of competing. You compete to win. Over time you will come to avoid contests where winning seems unlikely.

Competition action items:

- You may have a strong desire to win — to defeat an opponent of some sort. This motivation is common in the business world but not explicitly encouraged in education. In fact, as a teacher, you may feel uncomfortable leveraging this talent toward other people. But think about it this way: Your opponents don't have to be people; they can be issues. To clarify those issues, give them names. Compete against ignorance, student failure, poverty, boredom, or school dropouts. When you know your foe, you are apt to be more motivated and effective. When you find a way to use that talent, you will become a stronger educator.

- At heart, your competitive nature may be about your value of and need for comparison in your life. It's a way of ensuring that you achieve to your full potential. When you compare your performances with those of others, you become more motivated. Consider comparing your performance and results to those of another highly effective teacher. In doing so, you may push yourself toward a peak performance of your own.

- You instinctively understand the value of games and contests. You like them because there is always something at stake. Use your appreciation of games as a way to heighten the stakes in a classroom or even the entire school. Because in any contest some win and some lose, the first response of many people is to avoid contests and hurt feelings. However, for you, the real solution may be to create varied opportunities for students to compete. Keep creating educational contests so that eventually everybody can win at something.

- You know that progress must be measurable if it is to be meaningful. Your competitive talents could help you be a key contributor as your school establishes its measures of effectiveness and success. Use your talents to help your school determine the right educational benchmarks, and if you can, become part of the evaluative process. You are also uniquely poised to help students see those benchmarks as means rather than ends, allies rather than enemies, of learning. Many people are extremely uncomfortable at the thought of being scored. You yearn for it. Because you find comparison exhilarating, your contributions can be especially motivating.

- Comparison comes naturally to you. That's likely to be one of your greatest talents. When you compare one person's performance to someone else's, remember to consider the unique talents of those people. Understand that different talents lead to excellence in different areas. Remember that comparison is not always about competition. Sometimes comparison is best used to gain valuable insights to draw on as you teach.

- The National Football League has a celebration penalty, but there should be no such rule in a strengths-based school or classroom. Create a culture in which every significant victory or win (not just the athletic ones) by students or staff is speedily and predictably followed by a corresponding recognition and celebration. Make sure that all the winners and everyone who contributed to the victory get some credit — name names, make noise, and go home feeling like you scored big.

Competition in teachers sounds like this:

"I'm always in a contest with my peers. Can I do something better? Can I make a better lesson? Can I get through to non-compliant students? Can I get my test scores raised before they do? Can I be a better teacher than I was last year?"

"I want my students to succeed and exceed — to compete and win by surpassing the expectations of their parents and of the school — to the point of fulfilling their own potential."

Connectedness

Things happen for a reason. You are sure of it. You are sure of it because in your soul you know that we are all connected. Yes, we are individuals, responsible for our own judgments and in possession of our own free will, but nonetheless we are part of something larger. Some may call it the collective unconscious. Others may label it spirit or life force. But whatever your word of choice, you gain confidence from knowing that we are not isolated from one another or from the earth and the life on it. This feeling of Connectedness implies certain responsibilities. If we are all part of a larger picture, then we must not harm others because we will be harming ourselves. We must not exploit because we will be exploiting ourselves. Your awareness of these responsibilities creates your value system. You are considerate, caring, and accepting. Certain of the unity of humankind, you are a bridge builder for people of different cultures. Sensitive to the invisible hand, you can give others comfort that there is a purpose beyond our humdrum lives. The exact articles of your faith will depend on your upbringing and your culture, but your faith is strong. It sustains you and your close friends in the face of life's mysteries.

Connectedness action items:

- Educational institutions are diverse. Gender, age, race, and culture are the obvious markers, but there are numerous invisible ones, too. While everybody can spot the obvious human differences, you instinctively notice the similarities that unite people. You have the singular ability to see the hidden connections, even when the people in question can't. Remind people of the commonalities that you see so readily and that provide you with so much satisfaction. Once noticed, they have the potential for creating deep connections within educational communities.

- For some teachers, the classroom is everything. They may be so engaged in the classroom and their standard curriculum that they become somewhat isolated from the rest of the world. You're different. You see no boundaries to the education you provide. Look for opportunities to share and express your global perspective in your classroom and out of it. Because you see the connections that other people miss, you can help others discover meaning and purpose beyond compartmentalized worlds.

- Though you teach individual students, you probably have a natural interest in events that shape the whole of humanity. If this is the case for you, use your talents to explain important human issues and how they're relevant to your students and colleagues. Your efforts can lead to more effective and humane global citizenship — as well as helping young people understand their roles in a world beyond that which they see every day.

- Sometimes Connectedness talents are manifested as an interest in or concern about environmental matters. This interest could be in the educational, natural, scientific, social, or emotional ecologies and economies of the world — maybe all of them at once. Use your talents to teach your students how the little things people do, or don't do, have a lasting impact on the entire world. Use your Connectedness to explore how everyone on earth can affect everyone else.

The more tangible and quantifiable you make the lessons, the more powerful the learning and subsequent action will be.

- Because of your heightened appreciation for the global environment and the people in it, you might want to consider involvement in foreign exchange programs for students and/or teachers. If you can't visit other countries or host international students, try having visitors speak to your class. Take the class to museums when you have the chance. You have a natural insight into the ways different cultures and different eras are related, and you may find the experience refreshing. Capitalize on every opportunity that comes your way. You'll be a stronger teacher and enjoy your work more, and your students will grow beyond the expectations of many.

- You will probably never see students as simply minds that must be filled or blank slates that you have two semesters to fill. You tend to have a more holistic view of students — one that includes the interaction and integration of mind, body, spirit, emotions, relationships, society, and culture. When others are focused on only a small piece of the educational pie, their own bit to learn or subject to teach, you can help people become more aware of human complexity and how to integrate it.

Connectedness in teachers sounds like this:

"I can't see individual students, topics, or projects separately. I'm not good at compartmentalizing. Even as a little girl, I wanted to bring the people I knew together. In my mind, they just fit together, even if they couldn't see it themselves."

"I teach Spanish — not because of any personal history or cultural affinity, but because I love seeing how differences lead to sameness. I want to connect students not just to the material, but to each other."

Consistency

Balance is important to you. You are keenly aware of the need to treat people the same, no matter what their station in life, so you do not want to see the scales tipped too far in any one person's favor. In your view this leads to selfishness and individualism. It leads to a world where some people gain an unfair advantage because of their connections or their background or their greasing of the wheels. This is truly offensive to you. You see yourself as a guardian against it. In direct contrast to this world of special favors, you believe that people function best in a consistent environment where the rules are clear and are applied to everyone equally. This is an environment where people know what is expected. It is predictable and evenhanded. It is fair. Here each person has an even chance to show his or her worth.

Consistency action items:

- Many teachers are great because of their ability to customize. You're a little different: You are likely to be a great teacher because of your uncommon capacity to standardize. The predictable and reliable environment you create will be characterized by equality and efficiency. Your students will seldom be unpleasantly surprised; they will know exactly what is expected of them every day. Identify the key standard operating procedures that make your classroom a better place to learn. Think about how these procedures could be standardized more widely in your school, and come up with a plan that you could share with a school administrator or teaching colleague.

- Are some of the rules of your classroom "unwritten"? If so, "write" them. Rules are important tools in your mission to prevent favoritism and promote equality. Unwritten rules, as their very name describes, are often vague and are therefore inefficient and difficult to follow and apply. The rules of your classroom will always be most effective when your students have a perfect understanding of them and of the reasoning behind them.

- Because of your exceptional desire for consistency, you are also naturally aware of the variance among your students' learning styles. When you see the need, use your talents in a more detailed way by insisting on consistency between each student's learning style and the manner in which he or she is taught. That is what a level playing field really looks like: teaching that matches who the student really is.

- Your desire for consistency may make you an effective advocate for students who would be considered minorities in the student population. Consider joining organizations that support minority causes and equal opportunities for all students, regardless of their race, gender, or creed. Your awareness of and commitment to the need for equality in the midst of diversity can assist in the development of school policies that protect the students' rights, promote the value of each individual, and improve education in your school.

- Balanced and consistent, your even-keeled approach could have a calming and supportive effect on students who have lived much of their lives in chaotic and insecure environments. Your stable and solid approach to teaching could become a dependable foundation on which some of your students can start to rebuild their lives. Identify the students in your classroom who might fall into this category. Determine the types of stability and security that are most critical to their success in the classroom, and do your best to provide that support for them.

Consistency in teachers sounds like this:

"Individual fairness is important to me, but it has to be consistently applied to everyone, or it's not fair at all. Young people are really quick to spot unfairness. I love to level the playing field for each and every student so that they get an equal chance for success."

"Over the years, I've learned some things that work in the classroom, and I depend on them. I don't create new lesson plans in the middle of class."

Context

You look back. You look back because that is where the answers lie. You look back to understand the present. From your vantage point the present is unstable, a confusing clamor of competing voices. It is only by casting your mind back to an earlier time, a time when the plans were being drawn up, that the present regains its stability. The earlier time was a simpler time. It was a time of blueprints. As you look back, you begin to see these blueprints emerge. You realize what the initial intentions were. These blueprints or intentions have since become so embellished that they are almost unrecognizable, but now this Context theme reveals them again. This understanding brings you confidence. No longer disoriented, you make better decisions because you sense the underlying structure. You become a better partner because you understand how your colleagues came to be who they are. And counter intuitively you become wiser about the future because you saw its seeds being sown in the past. Faced with new people and new situations, it will take you a little time to orient yourself, but you must give yourself this time. You must discipline yourself to ask the questions and allow the blueprints to emerge because no matter what the situation, if you haven't seen the blueprints, you will have less confidence in your decisions.

Context action items:

- Your memory and appreciation of the past may be more developed than that of others. You have a unique ability to see the past as a prelude and understand what that means for the present and future. Share that wisdom with students who are ready to become more engaged in their education

101

by becoming aware of the connection between present efforts and future rewards.

- One of the benefits of Context talents for teachers is that you are better equipped to recall what it was like to be a student — academically, physically, emotionally, and socially. Use your capacity for understanding student contexts to create curricula and learning environments that take the student context into consideration.

- Considering your Context talents, it may be obvious that teaching some kind of history would be a logical choice for you. What may not be as obvious is how to bring the past into your classes that aren't noticeably history related. Learn about the history of math, science, physical education, music — whatever subject matter you teach. Capture the highlights, and use them in your teaching. Almost all students do better if they understand what the piece they're learning means, its ramifications, and how it fits into a wider scope — in other words, its context — which you are able to provide in spades.

- You might find that case studies are a natural teaching tool. Case studies involve using a historical event to teach current lessons. Think about how you can expand and extend the use of case studies in your classroom. Identify new sources of cases that will be relevant to your students and the curricula you teach. If you have access to a college library, you'll find that academic journals and textbooks are a goldmine for case studies.

- Your talents in chronology may make you the perfect archivist or historian for your school or district. Let people know that you love history and that preserving the past is an important value for you. If you can't be your school's historian, check into local historical societies. You'll find one in just about every town in the nation, and many of them would appreciate fresh blood and willing hands. The experience will give you valuable insights that you can bring to your classroom.

Context in teachers sounds like this:

"Every time I'm confronted with a new problem in the classroom, I think about how problems like it have been resolved before. It helps."

"It helps me so much to understand each student's life history. That way, I can understand how each part of their lives will affect their current learning experience."

Deliberative

You are careful. You are vigilant. You are a private person. You know that the world is an unpredictable place. Everything may seem in order, but beneath the surface you sense the many risks. Rather than denying these risks, you draw each one out into the open. Then each risk can be identified, assessed, and ultimately reduced. Thus, you are a fairly serious person who approaches life with a certain reserve. For example, you like to plan ahead so as to anticipate what might go wrong. You select your friends cautiously and keep your own counsel when the conversation turns to personal matters. You are careful not to give too much praise and recognition, lest it be misconstrued. If some people don't like you because you are not as effusive as others, then so be it. For you, life is not a popularity contest. Life is something of a minefield. Others can run through it recklessly if they so choose, but you take a different approach. You identify the dangers, weigh their relative impact, and then place your feet deliberately. You walk with care.

Deliberative action items:

- You buy into the wisdom that says "Haste makes waste." Because your students live in a 24/7 world, your way might cut against the grain of theirs. But you're right — healthy growth is not instantaneous; it takes time. Deliberative is a talent uniquely suited to a studied, unhurried approach, and there is tremendous value in that. While other educators might take a fast-track approach to learning, don't apologize for occasionally applying the brakes in your classroom. It gives your students time to let concepts take root and grow.

- You are unlikely to be careless or indiscriminate in handing out compliments. Consequently, your words of praise are likely to be highly prized by students and colleagues. While the value of your praise may be related to its rarity, consider how you might increase the frequency of praise without reducing or compromising its sincerity or validity. In other words, make a conscious effort to notice the achievements that might have slipped under your radar. A slight increase in your praise could result in dramatic improvement in the engagement of students and staff in your school.

- You instinctively seek to reduce risk by working to prevent problems. This is a valuable trait for a teacher because your classroom won't be volatile or chaotic. It makes students feel safe, and a student who doesn't feel safe probably won't learn. That doesn't mean everyone will understand your methodology, however. Whenever you raise a cautionary flag, be sure you can make it clear that what you're really doing is creating an environment that is more conducive to effective learning. You're trying to head off preventable problems at the pass.

- Your Deliberative talents may influence the way you form relationships. You will probably need more, not less, time to get to know your students and colleagues. There may not be enough time in the school day for you to achieve the kind of human connections you need to be effective in your role. If it takes you a little longer, you may need to start a little earlier. As a teacher, start getting to know your students before school even gets started, if you can. This kind of relational head start may provide you with the social foundation you need to hit the ground running on the first day of school.

- You are likely to require privacy — personally and at school. Because teaching is, by nature, quite public, you might need to deliberately carve out some time in the day to be by yourself. Better yet: If you can, co-opt a private place for yourself so you can have time alone when you need it. You might need to give your students and colleagues some simple cues that indicate your need for privacy.

Deliberative in teachers sounds like this:

"I like to take my time when I'm developing a lesson plan. You can't just throw one together if you want it to be effective."

"I tend to think things over pretty carefully when I'm selecting textbooks. I've never understood people who could just make snap decisions. Look before you leap!"

Developer

You see the potential in others. Very often, in fact, potential is all you see. In your view no individual is fully formed. On the contrary, each individual is a work in progress, alive with possibilities. And you are drawn toward people for this very reason. When you interact with others, your goal is to help them experience success. You look for ways to challenge them. You devise interesting experiences that can stretch them and help them grow. And all the while you are on the lookout for the signs of growth — a new behavior learned or modified, a slight improvement in a skill, a glimpse of excellence or of "flow" where previously there were only halting steps. For you these small increments — invisible to some — are clear signs of potential being realized. These signs of growth in others are your fuel. They bring you strength and satisfaction. Over time many will seek you out for help and encouragement because on some level they know that your helpfulness is both genuine and fulfilling to you.

Developer action items:

- Contributing to the growth of a student, or a peer for that matter, gives you great satisfaction. You might explain this feeling away by saying it's because you're a teacher. But you're not a developer because you're a teacher; you're a teacher because you're a natural developer of people. Recognize, value, and celebrate the wonderful fit between who you are as a person and what you get to do professionally every day.

- You are a natural encourager. It's likely that you are talented at noticing progress, no matter how tiny and incremental it might be. This ability gives you many opportunities to compliment people for progress they are making but that may have gone unnoticed. Your detailed observations will make the recipients feel important and worthwhile, so make a point of putting this talent to work.

- Some people become impatient and frustrated with "rookies." You, however, are probably very comfortable working with people who are inexperienced and unseasoned. Look for new teachers who possess raw teaching talents that need to be refined and seasoned, and invite them to be your protégés. Your willingness to share your experiential knowledge will be a powerful factor as these people develop strengths as teachers.

- It is never too early to start developing great teachers. Don't hesitate to share the work of teaching in your classroom with students who seem to have potential in this area. When you give them real opportunities to teach a class or help another student, you are giving them a taste of what it feels like to be actively involved in helping others grow. As you well know, the experience of contributing to human growth and learning can be very satisfying and even addictive. That sounds like a pretty good habit for some of your students to develop.

- Though it is your nature to support others, carefully avoid supporting a teacher who is consistently struggling because his or her talents don't fit the role. Granted, there will be situations in which helping an ineffective teacher do his or her job in a slightly different manner will be appropriate and helpful. But there will also be occasions when the best developmental action you can take is to help that person find a different role — a role that fits his or her greatest talents.

Developer in teachers sounds like this:

"I often notice students' progress before they do. And when I recognize their achievements, *they* are much more likely to recognize those achievements and to advance them even further."

"I can't tell you how much joy I find in helping young people develop. There's nothing like seeing students grow and become the people they were meant to be. I love it."

Discipline

Your world needs to be predictable. It needs to be ordered and planned. So you instinctively impose structure on your world. You set up routines. You focus on timelines and deadlines. You break long-term projects into a series of specific short-term plans, and you work through each plan diligently. You are not necessarily neat and clean, but you do need precision. Faced with the inherent messiness of life, you want to feel in control. The routines, the timelines, the structure, all of these help create this feeling of control. Lacking this theme of Discipline, others may sometimes resent your need for order, but there need not be conflict. You must understand that not everyone feels your urge for predictability; they have other ways of getting things done. Likewise, you can help them understand and even appreciate your need for structure. Your dislike of surprises, your impatience with errors, your routines, and your detail orientation don't need to be misinterpreted as controlling behaviors that box people in. Rather, these behaviors can be understood as your instinctive method for maintaining your progress and your productivity in the face of life's many distractions.

Discipline action items:

- You are naturally inclined to be prepared; you are likely to have a plan for everything that happens in your classroom. To you, learning is seldom something that just happens by chance or accident. Instead, you rely on foresight and preparation to create a classroom environment with structure and order. Make sure that you have adequate time to plan. If your planning period doesn't provide you with enough time, try to find another block of time in your day.

Flying by the seat of your pants probably won't feel good to you and won't get you the kind of results you want.

- You probably feel best when your surroundings are neat, clean, and well-kept. Because your students are likely to disrupt the order of your physical space, consider putting your room back in order at only one or two predetermined times during the day. That way, you know that it will be in order, but you won't be fighting a losing battle to keep it that way.

- Quality is often about the details. Your meticulous attention to details and timeliness make you a star at getting things done on time. Highly disciplined and organized people are probably in the minority in most organizations, which means that often, others will not match your promptness or detail orientation. To counteract this lack of discipline, you might want to build some "earliness" into the deadlines you give others so that your needs and expectations can be met.

- Efficiency is probably important to you. While most people understand that something needs to get done, they may still be unclear about the important details of who gets it done, how, and when. When you use your natural capacity for planning and establishing efficient routines, you organize and clarify the efforts of others. Remember that efficiency is also a function of matching talent to task. When the right people get involved in the routines you establish, the efficiency and the effectiveness of those routines will be amplified.

- Accurate and detailed records are important in educational institutions. You are likely to have a well-designed system to measure and monitor student performances. You've surely noticed that parents love this. Consider sharing what you've learned about keeping track of student data with other teachers. It can help them do a more effective job of evaluating and analyzing student performance.

Discipline in teachers sounds like this:

"I have several detailed systems that ensure we meet our objectives. Parents really like my progress reports."

"My principal has figured out that I have a lot of Discipline talent. Whenever she really needs something done, and she knows it will take a lot of structure and planning, she tends to pick me to do it."

Empathy

You can sense the emotions of those around you. You can feel what they are feeling as though their feelings are your own. Intuitively, you are able to see the world through their eyes and share their perspective. You do not necessarily agree with each person's perspective. You do not necessarily feel pity for each person's predicament — this would be sympathy, not Empathy. You do not necessarily condone the choices each person makes, but you do understand. This instinctive ability to understand is powerful. You hear the unvoiced questions. You anticipate the need. Where others grapple for words, you seem to find the right words and the right tone. You help people find the right phrases to express their feelings — to themselves as well as to others. You help them give voice to their emotional life. For all these reasons other people are drawn to you.

Empathy action items:

- How a student feels affects how he or she learns. Negative emotions — anger, fear, anxiety — limit learning, while positive emotions can pave the way for almost unlimited learning. You can pick up on these emotions without even trying. You have emotional radar that makes you sensitive to and aware of the emotions of others. Use your emotional intelligence to identify the emotions of your students and the class as a whole each day, and track those emotions over the course of a semester. See if you can discover emotional trends that contribute to educational progress or regress.

- You are highly sensitive to the emotions of the individuals you encounter — so sensitive, in fact, that you might begin to feel a sense of responsibility for those emotions. Be constantly aware that your best empathetic efforts will be brief connections, rather than extended emotional and personal ties. If an individual's emotions linger within you, or if you begin to feel personal responsibility for them, you may have crossed an emotional boundary.

- Sometimes people can be oblivious to the powerful emotional undercurrents of their lives, or they might have difficulty identifying and understanding them. You can help. Work at developing a more sophisticated emotional vocabulary. Move beyond *mad, sad,* and *glad* to find words that more adequately describe the richness and texture of human emotion. When you use these words to clearly communicate the emotions you see and feel in students, parents, and colleagues, you will help them understand their feelings and gain clarity about what it means to be a human being.

- Empathy tends to be associated with sensitivity to the painful emotions of others. Your natural wiring does put you in touch with negative emotions, but you need not and probably should not limit your radar to just bad feelings. Remember to include and reinforce the full range of human emotion, including positive emotions. "Happy" doesn't seem to require the immediate response of "miserable," but it deserves your attention, too.

- Your emotional intelligence is likely to play a key role in your teaching successes, as an individual and as a teaching partner. Not all of your teaching colleagues will have your emotional instincts and intuition. Some may be more logical and intellectual in their approach to education. Consider forming complementary partnerships with some of these colleagues. The joining of their smart thinking and your sensitive feelings will help to ensure that the "whole student" is being developed.

Empathy in teachers sounds like this:

"Sometimes, I have a sixth sense when I walk into the classroom for noticing how one particular student may be feeling. I seem to be able to sense feelings when others are unaware that they exist."

"If any of my students has a special need in the learning process, it's immediately obvious to me. I feel their confusion or frustration, and I work to alleviate it as quickly as possible. No student should be left to struggle through the learning process alone."

Focus

"Where am I headed?" you ask yourself. You ask this question every day. Guided by this theme of Focus, you need a clear destination. Lacking one, your life and your work can quickly become frustrating. And so each year, each month, and even each week you set goals. These goals then serve as your compass, helping you determine priorities and make the necessary corrections to get back on course. Your Focus is powerful because it forces you to filter; you instinctively evaluate whether or not a particular action will help you move toward your goal. Those that don't are ignored. In the end, then, your Focus forces you to be efficient. Naturally, the flip side of this is that it causes you to become impatient with delays, obstacles, and even tangents, no matter how intriguing they appear to be. This makes you an extremely valuable team member. When others start to wander down other avenues, you bring them back to the main road. Your Focus reminds everyone that if something is not helping you move toward your destination, then it is not important. And if it is not important, then it is not worth your time. You keep everyone on point.

Focus action items:

- Involvement in projects without specific goals or objectives will frustrate you — but there's a way to productively use that tension. Instead of getting mad, define outcomes, detail steps, set goals, and tell people what you've done. When you share your focus with your students and colleagues, you will substantially improve their chances of actually producing the outcome you've defined.

- There are times when school can be a very distracting place. The attention of your students may be diverted by the cacophony of the classroom or sidetracked by the chaos of interactions with their friends. Use your ability to concentrate in the midst of the distraction to regularly remind them of where they are headed and to repeatedly help them see the connection between today's behavior and tomorrow's results.

- You will be at your best as a teacher when you are aiming at a tangible educational target. It will act as a powerful magnet that pulls you toward accomplishment. The competing demands of everyday life can sometimes divert your attention and efforts, and for you, that can be frustrating. Write down your goals and objectives, and post them somewhere. These obvious reminders will create a greater sense of direction and accountability.

- Your capacity to concentrate so avidly might make you seem inaccessible and unapproachable. Let your students know that your occasional highly focused states of mind do not mean disinterest in other people. Make sure they know that they have permission to interrupt you whenever they want or need your attention.

- Some of your students may be completely unaware of their progress. Some people simply don't notice the milestones they've reached. You instinctively understand the incremental sequence that leads to an outcome, so you can see progress clearer than most. Look for opportunities to talk to students about their academic and personal progress. You might find a chance to celebrate success and create motivation for the rest of the journey.

Focus in teachers sounds like this:

"I set specific targets for my students, and I ensure that each lesson or activity is aimed at that target. It helps keep the educational process coherent and effective."

"I strive to allow myself and my students to focus on one thing at a time. Multi-tasking isn't all it's cracked up to be."

Futuristic

"Wouldn't it be great if . . ." You are the kind of person who loves to peer over the horizon. The future fascinates you. As if it were projected on the wall, you see in detail what the future might hold, and this detailed picture keeps pulling you forward, into tomorrow. While the exact content of the picture will depend on your other strengths and interests — a better product, a better team, a better life, or a better world — it will always be inspirational to you. You are a dreamer who sees visions of what could be and who cherishes those visions. When the present proves too frustrating and the people around you too pragmatic, you conjure up your visions of the future and they energize you. They can energize others, too. In fact, very often people look to you to describe your visions of the future. They want a picture that can raise their sights and thereby their spirits. You can paint it for them. Practice. Choose your words carefully. Make the picture as vivid as possible. People will want to latch on to the hope you bring.

Futuristic action items:

- It's no secret that students sometimes find the classroom monotonous and boring. Your orientation toward the future enables you to see beyond the routine of the present to a new and preferred future. Inspire your students by describing a tomorrow that is better than either yesterday or today. Let's face it: For many, learning is work, and work can get dull. Leavening work with inspiration brings meaning and purpose.

- Actively and frequently "dream" on behalf of and with your students. When you leverage your talents in anticipation and imagination, you sow seeds of better futures in the minds and hearts of your students. This is how poetry is conceived, how Olympic medals are won, how music gets written, how new companies are born, and how better mousetraps are invented. As students identify their preferred future, help them make it happen.

- Your capacity to see what is coming will often provide you with the wonderful advantage of having time to get ready for it. Identify possibilities that are just beyond the educational horizon, and share them with those who might benefit from your perspective on the future and get a head start.

- Your visions will be more effectively cast as you move from helping others see the future to helping others experience the future. Use vivid multisensory descriptors that go beyond the visual to include hearing, sensing, feeling, and being. The more you can help people feel what they're aiming for, the more likely they are to produce it.

- To really leverage your talents, be intentional about getting near those you want to influence and inspire. Just as a magnet becomes more powerful with close proximity, so too will your vision become more powerful and attractive when you move closer to those you hope will benefit from it.

Futuristic in teachers sounds like this:

"I often find myself envisioning a school that is very different from the one we have now. I can really see it."

"I like to paint a picture of a preferred future for young people who are feeling like life doesn't offer them much."

Harmony

You look for areas of agreement. In your view there is little to be gained from conflict and friction, so you seek to hold them to a minimum. When you know that the people around you hold differing views, you try to find the common ground. You try to steer them away from confrontation and toward harmony. In fact, harmony is one of your guiding values. You can't quite believe how much time is wasted by people trying to impose their views on others. Wouldn't we all be more productive if we kept our opinions in check and instead looked for consensus and support? You believe we would, and you live by that belief. When others are sounding off about their goals, their claims, and their fervently held opinions, you hold your peace. When others strike out in a direction, you will willingly, in the service of harmony, modify your own objectives to merge with theirs (as long as their basic values do not clash with yours). When others start to argue about their pet theory or concept, you steer clear of the debate, preferring to talk about practical, down-to-earth matters on which you can all agree. In your view we are all in the same boat, and we need this boat to get where we are going. It is a good boat. There is no need to rock it just to show that you can.

Harmony action items:

- For you, effective education probably isn't about the efforts of an individual student or teacher. Instead, you are likely to believe that great learning takes place in an environment that practices and values collaboration. Consider joining a teaching team. If such a team doesn't exist in your school, create one. The process will leverage your talents nicely, and the resulting team environment will make you a stronger teacher.

- By nature, you are probably more willing than others to rely on qualified experts. Intentionally think about the specific expertise you can supply and the expertise for which you will need to rely on others. That approach will clarify your thinking, and it will be valuable to any team of which you are a part. When every person on the team knows what they supply and on whom they rely, synergy and teamwork is enhanced.

- You are probably more interested in areas of agreement than in areas of disagreement. In your mind, the value of agreement far outweighs the costs that are incurred in a combat zone of disagreement. In the heat of an educational battle, step forward with your Harmony talents to unite divided and hostile opponents by reminding them of the common ground on which they stand.

- Your Harmony talents may make you more comfortable than most in the middle ground. This can make you the ideal moderator. Sooner or later, in every school, a situation of unproductive confrontation and conflict will arise. This can be your moment to shine. Consider jumping into the middle of the fray, not to add fuel to the fire, but to bring a fair and peaceful resolution.

- Harmony is not the same as unanimity. Harmony is not limited to one tone. It simply demands that different tones blend together to reduce dissonance. You are uniquely capable of pointing out that while solos may be beautiful, symphonies are made of blended voices. And the symphonies of teachers and students working together are magnificent.

Harmony in teachers sounds like this:

"We're going to a 'block schedule' next year. Some teachers are up in arms about it, but I'm looking at the bright side: If we all support this, maybe we can make it work. If it's inevitable, we need to at least come together and give it a try."

"If there's anything I can't stand, it's facing an upset parent."

Ideation

You are fascinated by ideas. What is an idea? An idea is a concept, the best explanation of the most events. You are delighted when you discover beneath the complex surface an elegantly simple concept to explain why things are the way they are. An idea is a connection. Yours is the kind of mind that is always looking for connections, and so you are intrigued when seemingly disparate phenomena can be linked by an obscure connection. An idea is a new perspective on familiar challenges. You revel in taking the world we all know and turning it around so we can view it from a strange but strangely enlightening angle. You love all these ideas because they are profound, because they are novel, because they are clarifying, because they are contrary, because they are bizarre. For all these reasons you derive a jolt of energy whenever a new idea occurs to you. Others may label you creative or original or conceptual or even smart. Perhaps you are all of these. Who can be sure? What you are sure of is that ideas are thrilling. And on most days this is enough.

Ideation action items:

- You have an open and creative mind. You naturally gravitate toward progressive concepts and approaches. If your school doesn't have an educational research and development team, consider starting one. You could lead or significantly contribute to a group that is committed to educational excellence through innovation. While much of your curriculum cannot be changed, you can apply your creative talents to the approach and style of your teaching.

All your students will benefit, especially those who are disengaged with the subject matter of the class.

- You have a natural ability to replace obsolete and irrelevant teaching approaches. Don't let it go to waste. Sometimes students get stuck in unproductive and even destructive ruts. They need to do things differently, but they have no idea how. You will become a valuable partner when you help these students invent new ways of approaching their schoolwork, relationships, or life in general.

- You bring great ideas to the table — but can you increase the quantity and quality of your ideas? Consider the circumstances under which you have produced your best ideas. When did you come up with these ideas? Identify the time of day, even the season. Where did you come up with them? Identify the physical locations. Did you conceive these ideas alone? Did the ideas emerge during conversations with others? If so, who are those people? By answering these questions, you might identify the human and physical environment in which you can maximize your Ideation talents.

- You have a natural capacity to consider issues from multiple perspectives. Not everyone in your school shares your talent to see different viewpoints. Consequently, you may be alone in your perspective on an issue or topic. That doesn't mean you're committed to it, just that you can see it, but others may not realize that. It's important that you make it clear that you're laying out a diversity of perspectives to be considered.

- While much of your curriculum cannot be changed, the approach and style of your teaching are perfect areas to apply your creative talents. Enliven students who are disengaged with the subject matter of the class by replacing an obsolete and irrelevant teaching approach with one that is new and completely "outside the book."

Ideation in teachers sounds like this:

"There's nothing that turns me on more than the opportunity to teach an entirely new concept."

"My colleagues would say creativity is a big part of me. It helps me tailor my lessons to individuals, and my lessons are always changing."

Includer

"Stretch the circle wider." This is the philosophy around which you orient your life. You want to include people and make them feel part of the group. In direct contrast to those who are drawn only to exclusive groups, you actively avoid those groups that exclude others. You want to expand the group so that as many people as possible can benefit from its support. You hate the sight of someone on the outside looking in. You want to draw them in so that they can feel the warmth of the group. You are an instinctively accepting person. Regardless of race or sex or nationality or personality or faith, you cast few judgments. Judgments can hurt a person's feelings. Why do that if you don't have to? Your accepting nature does not necessarily rest on a belief that each of us is different and that one should respect these differences. Rather, it rests on your conviction that fundamentally we are all the same. We are all equally important. Thus, no one should be ignored. Each of us should be included. It is the least we all deserve.

Includer action items:

- Includer is an extremely powerful talent socially. You could be a champion for social inclusion and against social exclusion. You are keenly and naturally aware of the pain that comes when someone gets left out and of the power that comes when everyone is included and involved. If groups in your school or district are accused of being cliquish, use your social sensitivity to help guide them toward greater inclusiveness.

- Your eyes often notice and your heart often feels for students who are marginalized or stigmatized for some reason. Become more intentional about actually reaching out to the "outsiders." Your genuine care and acceptance as a teacher can begin a young person's transformation from an outsider to an insider, from a disengaged student to a highly engaged student.

- Come up with ways to make everyone truly feel that they are an integral part of your classroom or school. What information should everyone have access to? What decisions could everyone have a say in? What events should everyone be invited to? How could you ensure that everyone receives some kind of individual recognition and appreciation? As this list expands, so will the circle of people who feel accepted, welcomed, and assimilated. These emotions are likely to have a positive impact on everyone's education.

- There may be times when you are uncomfortable with the recognition programs and the corresponding competition in your educational institution. In fact, you may be tempted to eliminate all such recognition because some people are excluded from it. Be careful not to overreact. Instead of eliminating recognition because it tends to exclude some, think of ways you could expand and multiply the opportunities for everyone to be recognized. Everyone does something for which they should be noticed and celebrated, and you're just the person to start the party.

- Because of your awareness of those who are outside some circles of life, you could be a key factor in the growth of a particular group or organization. Many times, an insider mentality limits the incorporation and assimilation of new people, and as a result, limits the infusion of new ideas, new strengths, and new energy that could expand the organization's potential and impact. Identify people who should be brought into the important work of education, and involve them. It could be as easy as inviting them to visit your classroom or asking them to get involved in an ad hoc committee at your school.

Includer in teachers sounds like this:

"My colleagues always ask me to help plan our get-togethers. I think it's because they know I'll find a way to get everyone involved, which makes everything more fun."

"Students think I'm a little strange sometimes because I'm so serious about making sure everyone is involved and asked to contribute. Every student feels valued in my classroom, and not every teacher can say that."

Individualization

Your Individualization theme leads you to be intrigued by the unique qualities of each person. You are impatient with generalizations or "types" because you don't want to obscure what is special and distinct about each person. Instead, you focus on the differences between individuals. You instinctively observe each person's style, each person's motivation, how each thinks, and how each builds relationships. You hear the one-of-a-kind stories in each person's life. This theme explains why you pick your friends just the right birthday gift, why you know that one person prefers praise in public and another detests it, and why you tailor your teaching style to accommodate one person's need to be shown and another's desire to "figure it out as I go." Because you are such a keen observer of other people's strengths, you can draw out the best in each person. This Individualization theme also helps you build productive teams. While some search around for the perfect team "structure" or "process," you know instinctively that the secret to great teams is casting by individual strengths so that everyone can do a lot of what they do well.

Individualization action items:

- In your mind, great teaching is not just a deep understanding of the curriculum, but it is also an equally deep understanding of each student. You might even study your students. Find colleagues who share your talents and your passion for customizing teaching, and invite them to a best-practice smorgasbord. Let everyone discuss what they do to understand and appreciate student uniqueness. It could take your teaching to a whole new level as it becomes even more tailored.

- You notice and appreciate the diversity of human personality. That tends to be an individualistic approach, but it has implications for collaborative and cooperative aspects of the educational enterprise. Use your knowledge about individuals to help create partnerships, teams, committees, and groups that really fit together. As you clarify the uniqueness of each person, you also bring clarity to how the individual pieces of the human puzzle fit together. Without your differentiation, the puzzle pieces will often remain unassembled and without synergy.

- The approach you take to teaching will depend on each student. It's not necessarily easier or more efficient than standardization, but it's your best way of helping students learn. For you, it works — but it won't for everyone. Use your Individualization talents as you evaluate other teachers. Just as you realized that each student has a naturally effective way of learning, be aware that each teacher has a naturally effective way of teaching. Explore and enjoy the diversity of teachers in your school. Maybe you could help get the best fit between teachers and students.

- You know that one size doesn't always fit all. You understand the value of offering choices to your students at school, but the range of choices might need your attention. In what areas should choice be limited — maybe curtailed? Where could a greater menu of choices be offered? Provide your students with more options, and help them make decisions that fit. As a result, they will probably feel greater owner-ship and will ultimately achieve greater success.

- When you come to school each day, do you feel like you must become a completely different person if you are to be accepted or to succeed? If you do, you should consider relocating to another environment — one in which your talents are more fully used and you don't need to change who you are. Your best teaching is likely to occur when you are surrounded by people who accept you and encourage you to become more of who you are.

Individualization in teachers sounds like this:

"Each student is unique. I have 30 10-year-olds in my class-room, and no two are the same."

"I always need to know the individual student first. Then I can teach him or her in a way that fits."

Input

You are inquisitive. You collect things. You might collect information — words, facts, books, and quotations — or you might collect tangible objects such as butterflies, baseball cards, porcelain dolls, or sepia photographs. Whatever you collect, you collect it because it interests you. And yours is the kind of mind that finds so many things interesting. The world is exciting precisely because of its infinite variety and complexity. If you read a great deal, it is not necessarily to refine your theories but, rather, to add more information to your archives. If you like to travel, it is because each new location offers novel artifacts and facts. These can be acquired and then stored away. Why are they worth storing? At the time of storing it is often hard to say exactly when or why you might need them, but who knows when they might become useful? With all those possible uses in mind, you really don't feel comfortable throwing anything away. So you keep acquiring and compiling and filing stuff away. It's interesting. It keeps your mind fresh. And perhaps one day some of it will prove valuable.

Input action items:

- You know that much of educational content is abstract and conceptual, so you look for physical things that can make a concept more real and understandable. You are naturally inclined toward the acquisition of tangible learning resources — stuff, and lots of it. When you come across some object, item, or material, your mind probably leaps to how it could be used in an educational way, so you hang on to it. Take inventory of the things you have gathered so you know exactly what you have to share (and so you can keep it to a manageable amount). Evaluate your system for making your tangible resources available to those who could benefit from them. Let students and teachers know what you have and how they can access it. Your resourcefulness will increase as you share your stuff with others. Plus, then you're free to accumulate more stuff.

- You may have an "input specialty." There may be a particular educational issue or topic that is of special interest to you and impels you to dig for more information and resources. It's not unusual for great teachers to become experts on specialized topics — and not necessarily in the discipline they teach. Let your administration know about your wealth of knowledge and resources in your input specialty, and offer to share the expertise you've gained because of your craving to know more.

- Many times, a school or a district faces a unique challenge or opportunity but lacks information. You might be the perfect researcher in these instances. Think about volunteering to gather information and relevant materials. Then make a presentation to the decision makers. Their decisions will be more informed and intelligent because of your input.

- Your love of information and your craving to know more may make the Internet irresistible to you. The problem is that fulfilling your need for input can be very time-consuming. Identify the sites that reliably cover what you need, mark them for future consumption, and think of them as you would the daily paper or a magazine. Read in temperate and timely doses, instead of huge gulps. You'll be faster and more productive, and it will be easier to refer others to your best sites.

Input in teachers sounds like this:

"I love filling the classroom with 'souvenirs': photos of class projects or items we collected during field trips. You never know when seeing one of those souvenirs will spark a learning moment for one of the students. I get the biggest kick when that happens."

"I had my husband build a storage closet for me in our basement. I use it to keep all kinds of materials I saved from my students' work. I don't know exactly when I'll need them, but someday, each piece will serve as the perfect illustration for future students."

Intellection

You like to think. You like mental activity. You like exercising the "muscles" of your brain, stretching them in multiple directions. This need for mental activity may be focused; for example, you may be trying to solve a problem or develop an idea or understand another person's feelings. The exact focus will depend on your other strengths. On the other hand, this mental activity may very well lack focus. The theme of Intellection does not dictate what you are thinking about; it simply describes that you like to think. You are the kind of person who enjoys your time alone because it is your time for musing and reflection. You are introspective. In a sense you are your own best companion, as you pose yourself questions and try out answers on yourself to see how they sound. This introspection may lead you to a slight sense of discontent as you compare what you are actually doing with all the thoughts and ideas that your mind conceives. Or this introspection may tend toward more pragmatic matters such as the events of the day or a conversation that you plan to have later. Wherever it leads you, this mental hum is one of the constants of your life.

Intellection action items:

- Your mind may be its most active and productive when you can be quiet and introspective. The classroom is seldom a quiet place, so be sure to carve out some still and silent time when you can be alone each day. It may be during your commute to work or at the end of the day after the last student has left the classroom. Such solitude will be fuel for your powerful mind.

- Your mind is always going. In fact, it may occasionally wake you in the middle of the night. Remember that although your thinking is continuous, your thoughts can be fleeting. Have a strategy for capturing your best thoughts. You might want to keep a journal (paper or electronic) on hand so you can easily convert your conceptual musings into black and white. That way, you will be able to revisit your thoughts and later refine them.

- Your thoughts, while obvious and apparent to you, may be imperceptible to others. As much as your students and colleagues might like to think as you do, they cannot read your mind. Be aware of the times when it is important to lift the shades of your mind and give others a glimpse of what's happening in your head. This may be especially true at staff meetings.

- Philosophical and theoretical discussions often draw you in and make you think deeply. Who are your best discussion partners? Who are the people who help you clarify and articulate your best thinking? Consider having a regular appointment with these key people. Think of it as your mind-sharpening session. It will be a lot of fun.

- You know how to develop great questions, and you enjoy asking them. Think about teaching as the discipline of raising important questions. Keep track of the questions that have stimulated the most discussion and generated the most learning. Keep asking these fruitful questions. As you prepare for each class you teach, identify the key question that you want your students to consider.

Intellection in teachers sounds like this:

"I live for class discussions. I love watching the wheels turn, and it gives me a lot to think about, too."

"There have been a lot of times I've missed the exit to my house on the way home from school. I just get caught up in my thoughts, and then I notice I've gone 10 miles past where I live. Cars are good for thinking."

Learner

You love to learn. The subject matter that interests you most will be determined by your other themes and experiences, but whatever the subject, you will always be drawn to the process of learning. The process, more than the content or the result, is especially exciting for you. You are energized by the steady and deliberate journey from ignorance to competence. The thrill of the first few facts, the early efforts to recite or practice what you have learned, the growing confidence of a skill mastered — this is the process that entices you. Your excitement leads you to engage in adult learning experiences — yoga or piano lessons or graduate classes. It enables you to thrive in dynamic work environments where you are asked to take on short project assignments and are expected to learn a lot about the new subject matter in a short period of time and then move on to the next one. This Learner theme does not necessarily mean that you seek to become the subject matter expert, or that you are striving for the respect that accompanies a professional or academic credential. The outcome of the learning is less significant than the "getting there."

Learner action items:

- Your large capacity for learning makes you the right person to study a challenging issue or problem facing education in general or your school in particular. It also makes you the right person to report what you've found to people who are responsible for taking action in those areas. Sometimes people take misguided steps or don't act at all simply because they don't know what to do. Use your Learner talents to inform and guide the response.

- As a learner, you are passionate about education. You love how it feels when you are on a steep learning curve, and you tend to get bored when you reach a learning plateau. Let others know that you enjoy the cutting edge and new frontiers, and volunteer to do exploration in these areas. You may be a key agent for change in your school. Other teachers might be intimidated by new ideas or new routines, but your willingness to soak up this newness can calm their fears and spur them to participate. Don't underestimate the positive effect you can have on them.

- Your Learner talents probably caused you to gravitate toward a career in education. You love to teach because you love to learn. Your best learning may often come when you accept the challenge of teaching something of importance to others. Your rich experience as a learner can enrich your practice of teaching. Keep expanding and extending the borders of your own intellect. In doing so, you will increase your effectiveness as a teacher.

- Because it is the process and experience of learning that you love, you may be unaware of the result — how you have grown as a person and a professional and the expertise you have acquired through your continuous studies. Take some time to identify your areas of expertise. Think about the conferences, seminars, or classes you have attended and the books you've bought in the past five years. Once you define your expertise, let others know that this is an area where you can help. In doing so, your learning will be put to work, and as you consult with others, you will learn even more.

- Consider making weekly entries in a "lessons learned journal." Because your mind is constantly in a state of exploration, the practice and structure of journaling could help capture and document your personal and professional discoveries. Writing down some of the content of your learning will have benefit for you and others. Your journal could become another book that you will want to study further, and it could be a source of wisdom and insight for others.

Learner in teachers sounds like this:

"I'm almost always reading a biography. I love learning 'nuggets' and bringing them into class. In reading a biography of Winston Churchill, I learned the origin of the word *posh*. When rich people sailed to India, they got to sit on the port side of the ship on the way there, and on the starboard side on the way home. So 'port out, starboard home: posh.' I just loved that!"

"I think I became a teacher because I know the thrill of learning. I love it, and I want young people to experience that same feeling of excitement."

Maximizer

Excellence, not average, is your measure. Taking something from below average to slightly above average takes a great deal of effort and in your opinion is not very rewarding. Transforming something strong into something superb takes just as much effort but is much more thrilling. Strengths, whether yours or someone else's, fascinate you. Like a diver after pearls, you search them out, watching for the telltale signs of a strength. A glimpse of untutored excellence, rapid learning, a skill mastered without recourse to steps — all these are clues that a strength may be in play. And having found a strength, you feel compelled to nurture it, refine it, and stretch it toward excellence. You polish the pearl until it shines. This natural sorting of strengths means that others see you as discriminating. You choose to spend time with people who appreciate your particular strengths. Likewise, you are attracted to others who seem to have found and cultivated their own strengths. You tend to avoid those who want to fix you and make you well rounded. You don't want to spend your life bemoaning what you lack. Rather, you want to capitalize on the gifts with which you are blessed. It's more fun. It's more productive. And, counter intuitively, it is more demanding.

Maximizer action items:

- Excellence and quality get your attention. That probably explains why you see talents and strengths in others, often before they do. You're well aware that fixing weaknesses just doesn't work, and your quality orientation could help to counteract the weakness-fixing mentality that many of your students will have. Provide your students with vivid descriptions of what they do well and of their unique potential.

- As one who has an appreciation of and an affinity for excellent performance, you may want to evaluate the time you spend working with your best performing students or classes. The demands of struggling students may have made it seem impossible to pay much attention to some of your best students. If this is the case, find ways to spend more time to work with your best students. With a little investment of your time and energy, your best student could quickly and easily become even better. This could be a wiser investment of your teaching time, and it could sustain you when you need to work with students whose progress is more limited.

- Because you instinctively seek to do more of what you naturally do best, you might be a good candidate for an educational specialty. Working with gifted students is an obvious possibility, but think broadly. Is there a particular area of education or teaching in which you have had significant success? Is there a subject in which you have great passion or expertise? Is there a possibility that you could work in this area full time? If you could choose to spend your time doing one thing, what would it be? Maybe you have more of a choice than you realize. Your engagement as a teacher will be highest when you are involved in those areas and activities in which you have been most successful.

- You are naturally a discriminating judge of performance. Your keen awareness of and preference for quality performances will often cause you to be drawn toward individuals who are the best performers. Be careful to avoid creating the perception that your discrimination about performance leads to discrimination about people. Try to move from noticing the best students in your class to noticing the best within each student. As a result, even more of your students will get an opportunity to benefit from your ability to maximize.

- Some might call you choosy or selective. Good. Though some may consider this a negative, good selections and wise choices are crucial to solid education. When decisions about who will be the best for a certain role need to be made, you should be involved. It will usually lead to a better outcome.

Maximizer in teachers sounds like this:

"One of my students in particular pays meticulous attention to detail. I always know that if I assign a really detail-oriented project, he will love the challenge and thrive on it."

"In grading papers or speeches, I look for examples of excellence and comment on them. I know that the positive feedback will encourage the student to perform at an even higher level. I include comments like 'Robert F. Kennedy would have loved your paragraph about how students can contribute to national issues like civil liberty. What do you think he would have added to it?' It helps students reach their potential, and it helps me fulfill what I feel is my role as a teacher."

Positivity

You are generous with praise, quick to smile, and always on the lookout for the positive in the situation. Some call you lighthearted. Others just wish that their glass were as full as yours seems to be. But either way, people want to be around you. Their world looks better around you because your enthusiasm is contagious. Lacking your energy and optimism, some find their world drab with repetition or, worse, heavy with pressure. You seem to find a way to lighten their spirit. You inject drama into every project. You celebrate every achievement. You find ways to make everything more exciting and more vital. Some cynics may reject your energy, but you are rarely dragged down. Your Positivity won't allow it. Somehow you can't quite escape your conviction that it is good to be alive, that work can be fun, and that no matter what the setbacks, one must never lose one's sense of humor.

Positivity action items:

- Encouraging people could be one of your greatest joys. Commit yourself to becoming increasingly liberal with your genuine praise of the people in your school. When you encounter something praiseworthy, immediately put your thoughts and feelings into words that can be heard or read. When you remind others of the positives you see, they are rewarded and encouraged, and so are you.

- You understand the critical link that exists between education and entertainment. Intentionally use your Positivity talents to create a classroom that is bright and stimulating and a social environment that is exciting and fun. Your students will learn more and faster because you have created a great place to go to school. They will show up each morning, not because they must, but because they want to.

- Let others know that your positive orientation is not the result of naiveté or ignorance of the negative. Help them understand that it's a natural and valid focus on the positive. Keep choosing the best, and ignore the rest. Your Positivity talents have the potential to improve the morale and possibly change the culture in your school.

- Not everyone knows how to throw a party. You do. Find frequent opportunities to celebrate something in your class-room. It could be a birthday, a new baby brother, a success in an extracurricular activity, the successful completion of a project, or simply TGIF. When you celebrate, you inject joy and drama into your students' psyches. When your students feel good, they are more apt to be good and do well.

- When you sense discouragement in students or staff, try to lift or lighten their moods. You can give people a lift when you remind them of the many good things that are happening. You get people to lighten up by injecting humor or rejecting seriousness. There are so many factors that pull people down. Your natural inclination toward the positive can be a much-needed remedy.

Positivity in teachers sounds like this:

"There is never a single morning on which I'm not excited about my job. As I leave for the school, I am absolutely certain that I will have an opportunity to make an important difference in the life of at least one student, and that thrills me!"

"When I was young, whenever I left the house, my mother reminded me to 'have a good time,' regardless of where I was going. That attitude helped me enjoy everything I did, and I can't resist passing on that good feeling by telling my students to enjoy the rest of the day whenever they leave my classroom."

Relator

Relator describes your attitude toward your relationships. In simple terms, the Relator theme pulls you toward people you already know. You do not necessarily shy away from meeting new people — in fact, you may have other themes that cause you to enjoy the thrill of turning strangers into friends — but you do derive a great deal of pleasure and strength from being around your close friends. You are comfortable with intimacy. Once the initial connection has been made, you deliberately encourage a deepening of the relationship. You want to understand their feelings, their goals, their fears, and their dreams; and you want them to understand yours. You know that this kind of closeness implies a certain amount of risk — you might be taken advantage of — but you are willing to accept that risk. For you a relationship has value only if it is genuine. And the only way to know that is to entrust yourself to the other person. The more you share with each other, the more you risk together. The more you risk together, the more each of you proves your caring is genuine. These are your steps toward real friendship, and you take them willingly.

Relator action items:

- As a talented Relator, you don't necessarily want to be close friends with everyone. You're probably most comfortable among people and in environments that let you be yourself. As an educator, your employee engagement might even require that you have a close friend at work because it will make you a better and happier teacher. If you are new at your school, look for a colleague who has the potential to become that friend.

- Your relationships are not superficial. They are deep and enduring, and they usually develop only with one-on-one interactions over time. Given the opportunity, you will often develop unusually close and caring human connections. Take the time to directly interact with each student in your classroom as much as you can. When your students know you as a person and you know them as individuals, you'll add a powerful human aspect to your teaching. It will be good for you and your students.

- Because you need time to get to know people, and because your greatest effectiveness may come through close and caring connections, consider teaching the same group of students for more than one school year. Instead of starting from a relational zero every year, move with your class to their next grade. If you can do it, it will be a great way to leverage your Relator talents.

- Relators tend to give more than they take — it's just how they operate. Don't forget that this is a form of real generosity, and for it to continue, you must ensure that your educational input keeps up with your educational output. If you don't have any classes to teach in the summer, use that time to fill your own reservoir. Relators need to make sure they aren't tapped out at the beginning of a school year.

- You're probably more comfortable with informal, rather than formal, systems and environments. Schools that are growing in size and complexity are likely to have more formalized systems. As these formalized structures increase, ensure that your need for informal systems continues to be nurtured.

Relator in teachers sounds like this:

"I like to contribute in extracurricular activities, but I really prefer to do it in small groups or even in a one-on-one situation rather than on a big committee. I feel much more involved and effective when there are just a few of us."

"It is important that I have one-on-one time with my students so I will get to know them. It's nice when I can share with them who I am, too."

Responsibility

Your Responsibility theme forces you to take psychological ownership for anything you commit to, and whether large or small, you feel emotionally bound to follow it through to completion. Your good name depends on it. If for some reason you cannot deliver, you automatically start to look for ways to make it up to the other person. Apologies are not enough. Excuses and rationalizations are totally unacceptable. You will not quite be able to live with yourself until you have made restitution. This conscientiousness, this near obsession for doing things right, and your impeccable ethics, combine to create your reputation: utterly dependable. When assigning new responsibilities, people will look to you first because they know it will get done. When people come to you for help — and they soon will — you must be selective. Your willingness to volunteer may sometimes lead you to take on more than you should.

Responsibility action items:

- Because of your dependable track record as a teacher, you'll probably be offered more and more roles and responsibilities. First, remember to take these offers as compliments. Second, remember to resist your initial impulse to say yes. Remind yourself that if you say yes to something when your schedule is already full, it probably means that you'll have to say no to an existing responsibility by default. It's not easy for people like you who feel responsible for everything to do this, but it will help in the long run.

- Schools are places of learning and growth. Your heightened awareness of right and wrong could position and prepare you to make significant contributions to the ethical and moral development of students. If you haven't already done so, consider taking a graduate class that focuses on ethical and moral development. The knowledge you'll gain will go a long way toward building a strength based on your Responsibility talents.

- Your exceptional Responsibility talents are likely to enhance your ability to respond to the needs and requests of others. Because that response gives you satisfaction and energy, you are often compelled to say yes — possibly too often. A team of people you trust that can help you evaluate requests might be helpful to you.

- You naturally take ownership of everything that involves you. As an owner, you are instinctively serious and dedicated to honoring your commitments. Because ownership of responsibility is your default setting, you may need to be more intentional about sharing responsibility. When you release some of your responsibilities to peers or students, remind yourself often that allowing others to help provides them with experiences that will contribute to their growth and development.

- Your Responsibility talents may make you acutely aware of performance standards and ethics. You want things to be done and done right. While you may know what you mean by "done right," others may not. Regularly define and describe what doing things the right way means — for the people you teach as well as the people with whom you teach. When you communicate and clarify your standards, others will be more likely to accept and live up to them.

Responsibility in teachers sounds like this:

"I believe in rules. If there's a rule, there's a reason. To some, that might seem a bit 'over the top,' but why are teachers required to follow a certain curriculum? To ensure that the students will get the knowledge they need for success. Why should students be quiet in class? Because they have a responsibility to each other to help create an effective learning environment."

"I feel such strong ownership of students' learning. I'm always amazed when people say, 'You put it out there; they should learn it.' Meeting in the middle is no way to do it; everyone should try to go the entire distance."

Restorative

You love to solve problems. Whereas some are dismayed when they encounter yet another breakdown, you can be energized by it. You enjoy the challenge of analyzing the symptoms, identifying what is wrong, and finding the solution. You may prefer practical problems or conceptual ones or personal ones. You may seek out specific kinds of problems that you have met many times before and that you are confident you can fix. Or you may feel the greatest push when faced with complex and unfamiliar problems. Your exact preferences are determined by your other themes and experiences. But what is certain is that you enjoy bringing things back to life. It is a wonderful feeling to identify the undermining factor(s), eradicate them, and restore something to its true glory. Intuitively, you know that without your intervention, this thing — this machine, this technique, this person, this company — might have ceased to function. You fixed it, resuscitated it, rekindled its vitality. Phrasing it the way you might, you saved it.

Restorative action items:

- Educational diagnosis may be one of your strengths. Instinctively, you spot flaws that limit academic achievement. This capacity to diagnose your students' educational obstacles and limitations will be most effective when you also help them find the remedies and antidotes for what ails them. Just as you have an eye for flaws, you also have the potential to see solutions. Try to offer a solution for every flaw you expose. In doing so, you can be a catalyst to true restoration.

- You are probably an excellent educational troubleshooter. Consider volunteering to take on the class that has had a negative and problematic reputation, and make it your goal to turn things around for the class and each student. There is no such thing as a school without problems. Let your school administration know that you love to solve problems and that you would be willing to serve on an ad hoc committee to deal with the thorniest challenges facing the school.

- Some people have a hard time hearing bad news. You cope better than most because problems and the people who tell you about them don't intimidate you. Let your students and their parents know that you appreciate brutal honesty and that it's okay to tell you when something isn't working. They'll feel more valuable because you listened to their opinions, and you'll be alerted to the critical issues that need attention and the puzzling problems that need to be solved.

- Fixing things comes easily for you, and you are drawn toward solving problems. However, remember that sometimes the best way to fix a problem is to empower people to fix it themselves. At times, it might be wise for you to fight the instinct to rush in and make everything better. Instead, assume the role of a problem-solving coach who encourages and instructs from the sidelines but ultimately allows students to find their own solutions and learn the valuable lessons that come from that process.

- You are likely to be your own harshest critic. You will usually be very aware of your flaws and failures as a teacher, and you will look for ways to overcome your weaknesses and eliminate your deficiencies. In fact, you might not be particularly comfortable with feedback about your strengths as an educator. Remember that your affinity for brutal honesty includes the truth about the ways you are strong and effective as a teacher. Don't write off your greatest abilities. They are the honest truth.

Restorative in teachers sounds like this:

"I like to solve students' problems. I'm good at it because I can usually see the sore spot. But at the same time, I have to back off a bit. If you always fix their problems, they never learn to do it themselves."

"I think it's important to manage my weaknesses as a teacher. I don't like knowing there's something I'm bad at — a way that I'm letting down my students — and not doing anything to remedy it."

Self-Assurance

Self-Assurance is similar to self-confidence. In the deepest part of you, you have faith in your strengths. You know that you are able — able to take risks, able to meet new challenges, able to stake claims, and, most important, able to deliver. But Self-Assurance is more than just self-confidence. Blessed with the theme of Self-Assurance, you have confidence not only in your abilities but also in your judgment. When you look at the world, you know that your perspective is unique and distinct. And because no one sees exactly what you see, you know that no one can make your decisions for you. No one can tell you what to think. They can guide. They can suggest. But you alone have the authority to form conclusions, make decisions, and act. This authority, this final accountability for the living of your life, does not intimidate you. On the contrary, it feels natural to you. No matter what the situation, you seem to know what the right decision is. This theme lends you an aura of certainty. Unlike many, you are not easily swayed by someone else's arguments, no matter how persuasive they may be. This Self-Assurance may be quiet or loud, depending on your other themes, but it is solid. It is strong. Like the keel of a ship, it withstands many different pressures and keeps you on your course.

Self-Assurance action items:

- Motivation is an internal thing for you. You really don't rely on others for either support or direction. This makes you particularly effective in situations that require independence in thought and action. Look for places in your school system that need and value that kind of independence. When you are given the freedom and autonomy, you will thrive.

- Even though you don't need the endorsement of others, there may be a contagiousness to your self-confidence. Consequently, others will attribute to you an authoritative credibility, and they will want to understand the rationale behind your certainty. Some people will share your certainty only when you explain the factors behind your convictions. Be prepared to share your reasoning. People who require empirical evidence need to follow your logic before they can follow you.

- Your teaching is probably rather intuitive. Sometimes your instincts lead you to unorthodox approaches, and your teaching may be misunderstood or unappreciated. Make a conscious effort to demonstrate that, though your methods are different, your educational outcomes are the same or better. When your colleagues are clear about the substance of your teaching, they may be more open to exploring the value and possible integration of your approach into more conventional educational practices.

- Challenges interest you because of their inherent risk and because they test your mettle. Challenges give you the opportunity to discern the right course of action, and they ultimately allow you to prove to yourself that you have worth and value as a human being. Identify an educational mountain that many have failed to scale or an educational gap that many have failed to bridge, and then start climbing and building. The challenge will bring out the best in you, and even more importantly, significant educational progress will occur.

- When you are personally and totally convinced of the value of something, your commitment will be enthusiastic and complete. When you are not personally convinced of the value, you will not hesitate to be seen as a member of a non-adopting minority. When involved in school politics, let others know what it takes to get your vote. It may be tough to get, but once you are won over, you are certain to be an assertive and instrumental ally.

Self-Assurance in teachers sounds like this:

"I don't spend much time second-guessing my lesson plans. If I know I'm right, I know I'm right."

"Some teachers tell me that they have butterflies in their stomachs every time they introduce themselves to a new class. I can understand their feelings, but at the same time, that's not the way it is for me. I always know that I've done it before and that I can do it again."

Significance

You want to be very significant in the eyes of other people. In the truest sense of the word you want to be recognized. You want to be heard. You want to stand out. You want to be known. In particular, you want to be known and appreciated for the unique strengths you bring. You feel a need to be admired as credible, professional, and successful. Likewise, you want to associate with others who are credible, professional, and successful. And if they aren't, you will push them to achieve until they are. Or you will move on. An independent spirit, you want your work to be a way of life rather than a job, and in that work you want to be given free rein, the leeway to do things your way. Your yearnings feel intense to you, and you honor those yearnings. And so your life is filled with goals, achievements, or qualifications that you crave. Whatever your focus — and each person is distinct — your Significance theme will keep pulling you upward, away from the mediocre toward the exceptional. It is the theme that keeps you reaching.

Significance action items:

- Teaching is an exceptionally good fit for you because you probably like being in front of an audience. You are uniquely comfortable with the pressure of public scrutiny and attention. Consider using your talents as a spokesperson who promotes the significant role and impact of teachers in our society. Your willingness to take this platform could contribute to raising the status of and support for the teaching profession.

- You are likely to have a strong and positive image in your school. This is no accident. You want people to see you in a positive light, and you consistently act in a manner that maintains and builds your image as a successful person and credible professional. Continue to monitor and improve your image as a teacher. While you are certainly much more than a public persona, some students will never get to experience the more substantive parts of you if they don't like what they first saw and experienced. When students see their teacher as someone they actually like, they are more apt to learn.

- You understand the value of applause, appreciation, and affirmation. In fact, you not only understand it, you need it. Who is your most significant audience? Make sure they understand the value you put on their perceptions and the important role they play in your continuing motivation. Their appreciation will lift you to ever-higher levels of accomplishment.

- You will probably be most effective and comfortable in educational environments that offer you some freedom and autonomy. You like these situations because the accomplishments will be yours alone — the result of your efforts and impact. The classroom is a perfect place to use these talents. While there is likely to be some outside influence, you will generally be in charge of what happens. Use your freedom as a teacher to do what needs to be done for your students.

- Your desire to be seen as successful and credible can help you be a great teacher. A successful and credible teacher is one who has successful and credible students. If you want to be seen as a great teacher, do great things for your students. While your personal ambitions and aspirations may seem somewhat self-centered, they can be the source of benefits for the students in your classroom. You won't be a great teacher until you are great to your students.

Significance in teachers sounds like this:

"As a teacher, I help students know that the subjects they learn in my classroom are the most important subjects in the world."

"My students love to receive compliments from me. They know that when I am impressed, they are doing exceptionally well."

Strategic

The Strategic theme enables you to sort through the clutter and find the best route. It is not a skill that can be taught. It is a distinct way of thinking, a special perspective on the world at large. This perspective allows you to see patterns where others simply see complexity. Mindful of these patterns, you play out alternative scenarios, always asking, "What if this happened? Okay, well what if this happened?" This recurring question helps you see around the next corner. There you can evaluate accurately the potential obstacles. Guided by where you see each path leading, you start to make selections. You discard the paths that lead nowhere. You discard the paths that lead straight into resistance. You discard the paths that lead into a fog of confusion. You cull and make selections until you arrive at the chosen path — your strategy. Armed with your strategy, you strike forward. This is your Strategic theme at work: "What if?" Select. Strike.

Strategic action items:

- Possibilities that are invisible to others are often obvious to you. While some people see only the road immediately in front of them, you are often able to see the multiplicity of routes that lead to a particular destination. This ability to see all the available options could be very valuable to students who are making important decisions about the direction of their lives. Share your wide-angled perspective with students who are at critical junctures in their lives. You will help them see that there are many more choices available and that the best one may still be out there.

- You are quite aware that new ventures should not be attempted without adequate planning and preparation. Let those who are responsible for new ventures in your school or district know that you can be a helpful resource on the front end of such an enterprise. Offer your talent for seeing the broad range of options that is available as well as your capacity for sorting through those options until you find the best route for moving forward. Strategic thinking at the beginning of an educational enterprise increases the probability of a good result.

- Your intelligence likely focuses on future possibilities. You're captivated by the what-ifs that lie ahead. Find educational dreamers or visionaries, and help them chart paths that will transform their dreams into reality. The ability to do this is more valuable than you might realize.

- For you, teaching plans are never static, fixed routines. You seldom will want to teach the same lesson in exactly the same way. Instead, you enter the classroom with a collection of alternatives and choices that can be made, depending on the unique educational environment and demands. Others may see your creative approach to teaching as simply flying by the seat of your pants. If you partner with colleagues who are more orderly and organized in their approach to teaching, help them see that the value of your teaching comes from its freshness and relevance.

- You may have an exceptional capacity for anticipation and imagination. Get involved in opportunities to determine the future direction of your school or district. Your open and creative mind might equip you to facilitate discussions and forums that will lead to an even brighter future.

Strategic in teachers sounds like this:

"I like to give writing assignments in which students need to come up with multiple endings to the story. That really expands their imagination."

"I never quite know how a discussion might go in my classroom, so I always have options for which direction we might take for the assignment that follows."

Woo

Woo stands for winning others over. You enjoy the challenge of meeting new people and getting them to like you. Strangers are rarely intimidating to you. On the contrary, strangers can be energizing. You are drawn to them. You want to learn their names, ask them questions, and find some area of common interest so that you can strike up a conversation and build rapport. Some people shy away from starting up conversations because they worry about running out of things to say. You don't. Not only are you rarely at a loss for words; you actually enjoy initiating with strangers because you derive satisfaction from breaking the ice and making a connection. Once that connection is made, you are quite happy to wrap it up and move on. There are new people to meet, new rooms to work, new crowds to mingle in. In your world there are no strangers, only friends you haven't met yet — lots of them.

Woo action items:

- You are blessed with social speed. You need to talk. You need to make friends with everyone. You need to make people like you. And you have the talent to do all those things very well. Think about how you can do a little more of what you do naturally and best. Could you measure your social speed? Do you know how many people you interact with in a typical day? How many social interactions do you have with students, parents, colleagues, administrators, or support staff? Increasing your interactions will be satisfying for you and good for your career and students.

- Social initiative most likely comes naturally for you. It's probably easy for you to initiate conversations and create a human connection. Your social instincts can serve you well, especially in educational situations that involve newcomers and strangers — your Woo becomes especially relevant around new people. Intentionally make the most of your talents during teacher orientation, the first day of class, and parent-teacher conferences. Your ability to make friends out of strangers will shine.

- Schools are often places that emphasize the value of what a person knows. However, as your Woo talents lead you to know, there are occasions on which who you know matters more than what you know. Like it or not, your educational efforts are often affected by political factors. You might want to consider getting more involved in the political realms that have an impact on your work as a teacher. Your ability to win others over could assist in creating policies and securing resources that are critical to educational effectiveness. Don't underestimate the power of your social intelligence and your capacity for building a broad and diverse constituency.

- Your desire to be liked as a person leads to the fact that you're a likeable person. If your students like being around you, they are probably less likely to look for reasons to miss class. If your students like you, they are probably more likely to listen to you and ultimately, to learn from you. Teaching is not a popularity contest, but your personal charisma and charm should be seen as a service to education. Is there a particular student who has been a challenge to you? Remember that more flies are caught with honey than vinegar.

- Remembering people's names may be one of the benefits of your Woo — one that many people envy. Be more intentional about using the names of your students and colleagues. How often do you incorporate student names in a typical class session? Does each of your students hear you say his or her name in a day? A week? A semester? What percentage of the students in your school could you name? Is it 25%? 50%? 75%? Increase that percentage, and increase your engagement and that of the students.

Woo in teachers sounds like this:

"Not striking up conversations with new students actually causes me stress — and talking brings young people out of their shells. I look for what we have in common so we can automatically be friends, because we're going to be friends."

"Some of my colleagues just can't relate to my need to make friends with every teacher, staff member, and administrator in the school. On the other hand, if the teachers need to make a request of the administration, I'm the one who'll be asked to represent the group. They know I'll get it done when the administration needs to be won over."

Chapter Five

Where Do You Go From Here?

L earning to use your talents is a journey of a thousand steps. By now, you've learned how your brain developed its talents, what they are, how to build on them in strengths development, and how to use them in the classroom. There's one last thing to know before you begin your strengths journey, and it may be the most important insight we share with you: You'll spend the rest of your life learning how to use your talents.

The first step of the journey is being aware of your talents, and the rest of the journey is learning to own and apply them. Every day will bring new challenges, new opportunities, and new ways to understand how to use your talents. As educators, we promote the power of lifelong learning, but perhaps nowhere will that be more important than in strengths development. In this chapter, you'll find a few ideas for using and capitalizing on your talents.

Some key ideas to remember:

Beware of the isolationist view. Your talents are complex. Using them in concert is even more complex, but with that complexity comes even greater opportunity for strength. So when you're tempted to focus on the talents from only one of your top themes or to think of each theme as being useful in only certain contexts, don't do it. Talents from all themes work together; they create their own unique dynamics in every situation. Your greatness is really a result of your ability to understand, embrace, and maximize your talents as they intermingle. In the same way that no single strength makes you a great teacher, no one theme of talent defines you. In essence, you are defined by *all* of your talents — *all* of the ways in which you naturally think, feel, and behave.

Find strengths in numbers. You'll be able to maximize your talents — and your strengths will reach the highest level of effectiveness — in an environment that finds and celebrates the talents of everyone. Michael Jordan once said that great players win games, but great teams win championships. It's true. You can accomplish a lot by using your talents, but your accomplishments will be narrower than they could be. When people partner their talents with those of others, they create an even more powerful dynamic.

Partnering talents, however, takes a special kind of reciprocity. Successful and satisfying human partnerships occur when the partners realize that each partner brings unique, necessary talents to the partnership. When you understand your talents, you know what you can provide to others. When you understand the talents of others, you become more able, perhaps more willing, to receive the best of what others have to offer.

And a word about your lesser talents: Don't waste time or energy trying to "fix" them. It's surprising how quickly some people revert to dwelling on what's wrong with them, even after discovering the tremendous potential of their greatest talents. Avoid the trap. Develop what you naturally do best. Success is always about what you've got, never about what you are not.

Starting Your Strengths Journey

All of this looks good on paper. The trick is moving from good idea in theory to great idea in practice. Here are some concrete suggestions for starting your strengths journey. Some are most applicable in a school that already embraces and uses strengths theory, but you might find that they all can be modified for your own situation.

- Write a personal mission statement describing your purpose in life and at work. Create a list of your values. Think about how you can use your talents to follow your values and fulfill your personal mission.

- Think about working with a mentor or strengths coach. Often, the best development opportunities are found in one-on-one relationships.

- Review and analyze your successes. Give some thought to your working partnerships and teams — especially the highly effective ones. Notice how your collective talents work together and why they are so effective. This will help you spot your talents in action and detect the talents of your partners.

- Identify three people who are important to your personal development and the fulfillment of your role. Using your top themes as a starting point, talk with these people, and discuss how, as a group, you can combine your talents to create greater successes.

- When preparing your agenda each day, consider your talents. Think about how you can best use them to accomplish each task. Don't forget to think about the skills and knowledge you can add to your talent to build strengths.

- You may know of challenges that await you this school year. You'll certainly face some you weren't expecting. As you meet these challenges, think of how your talents will serve you and with whom you need to partner to be successful.

- Consider how you can tap into your Signature Themes to accomplish your yearly goals in your classroom. Be specific about how to embrace your talents in each of those themes to meet your goals.

- The use of symbols and icons in an environment is incredibly important. (Don't think so? Imagine what would happen if the room number signs fell off the doors). Think about what symbols or reminders you can place around your classroom or your building that will remind everyone that the language of strengths is spoken in your school. Display teachers' Signature Themes on their doors.

- Begin each meeting with a short focus on strengths. Get creative about the types of questions you ask, but the simplest can be the most illuminating: Ask everyone about the strengths in which they used their greatest talents recently, how they expect to use those talents to deal with an upcoming situation, and if they need a partner with a complementary talent.

- Think about your students' talents. How can you find their best learning styles? How can you help students understand that they have talents that can lead to greatness?

Before You Go . . .

This self-awareness will have a greater and wider effect than you may now realize. The more you think about your talents, the more you'll notice how they contribute to your strengths. And the more you notice this connection, the more aware you'll be of your potential for even more strengths as a teacher.

Suzanne observed the impact of this self-awareness the first time she met her daughter's third-grade teacher, Mrs. Bell. "Elizabeth did okay in first and second grade, but her teachers never seemed to really help her progress significantly or help her have the kind of confidence that would propel her toward success in a sometimes cruel world," Suzanne says. But when Elizabeth started third grade, she seemed like a different person when she came home from school. Elizabeth was opening up more, talking about the details of her day, showing her mom her homework, making friends. "Even the way she walked home from school seemed different. She had more bounce to her step," Suzanne says.

Suzanne didn't make the connection between Elizabeth's new behavior and Mrs. Bell until the first parent-teacher conference. As Mrs. Bell showed Suzanne several examples of Elizabeth's math and language assignments, she kept saying, "Isn't this great work? Do you realize how well Elizabeth did on this particular assignment?"

After a while, Suzanne interrupted Mrs. Bell: "I told her, 'I'm just waiting for the *but*.' All her other teachers would say nice things, then say, '*But* Elizabeth really needs to work on this or that,' or '*But* we need to focus on some of her challenges,' or '*But* there are some weaknesses that should have some attention now.' There was always a *but*." Mrs. Bell, however, wasn't like the other teachers. "She said that there were no 'buts' in her classroom. She focused on what Elizabeth does well — her greatest talents — and promised Elizabeth would progress much more quickly," Suzanne says.

And she did. So much so that Suzanne thinks her best parenting was during Elizabeth's third-grade year because it was Elizabeth's best year — and that it was the result of Mrs. Bell's strengths. "I believe Mrs. Bell herself was not afraid to walk her talk and embrace her own talents in teaching. She knew how to take her best teacher self and use it over and over again in many different strengths. She knew how to make my daughter believe in herself by throwing out the *buts* and focusing on her talents," Suzanne says.

Mrs. Bell had never heard of strengths theory, probably didn't know she had unique talents, and certainly had no idea that the Clifton StrengthsFinder existed. Nonetheless, Mrs. Bell is a perfect example of strengths in action.

Knowing your talents and using them as the basis for strengths development will make you a better teacher, and our educational system needs more great teachers like Mrs. Bell. She may not have known about strengths theory, but you do. Our society can't afford to lose one more great teacher or pass over good teachers who could be great if they just made the most of their innate abilities. That's the reason we wrote this book. And the reason you are reading it? It's because you're the kind of teacher who feels compelled to get better and better at what you do. We feel compelled to help you do it.

Gallup has spent decades studying great teachers. Some of the best minds in the world have analyzed these teachers and their effects on education in general and students in particular. This massive, concerted, and unprecedented research has demonstrated what you may have suspected for a long time: Great teachers are the most valuable professionals in our society. At the very least, they provide our young people with the education they need to be successful adults. Sometimes, these great teachers even save young people who have no one else.

Great teachers want more than anything to have a significant impact on students' lives. They *have* to leave a mark, not only on students one by one, but also on the entire society. Embracing the idea that talents are the basis of strengths enhances lives, of course, but it also helps teachers leave that mark. Because teachers — and students — are so vitally important, we feel that it is imperative for educators to have the tools they need to be the best they can be. We hope that you use the tools provided in these pages to be the best you can be. You deserve it, and so do your students.

LEARN MORE

Gallup's staff development opportunities help school leaders, teachers, staff, and students discover their strengths and use them at school and in life.

To learn more about building a strengths-based school:

- Call Gallup's Education Division at 402-951-2003.

- Contact us by e-mail at twys@gallup.com.

- Visit our Web site at http://education.gallup.com.

- Subscribe to the *Gallup Educator,* Gallup's Education Division's online journal, at http://education.gallup.com/educator/.

REFERENCES

Clifton, D.O. & Nelson, P. (1992). *Soar with your strengths*. New York: Delacorte Press.

Coffman, C. & Gonzalez-Molina, G. (2002). *Follow this path: How the world's greatest organizations drive growth by unleashing human potential*. New York: Warner Books.

Goldhaber, D. (2002, Spring). The mystery of good teaching [Electronic version]. *Education Next, 2*, 50-55.

Hurlock, E.B. (1925). An evaluation of certain incentives used in school work. *Journal of Educational Psychology, 16*, 145-149.

National Education Association. (August 2003). *Status of the American public school teacher 2000-2001*. Retrieved January 17, 2005, from http://www.nea.org/edstats/images/status.pdf

Rose, L.C. & Gallup, A.M. (2002). *The 34th annual Phi Delta Kappa/Gallup poll of the public's attitudes toward the public schools*. Retrieved June 13, 2005, from http://www.pdkintl.org/kappan/k0209pol.htm

Rosenthal, R. (1998, Fall). Covert communication in classrooms, clinics, and courtrooms [Electronic version]. *Eye on Psi Chi, 3*, 18-22.

Sanders, W.L. & Rivers, J.C. (1996). *Cumulative and residual effects of teachers on future student academic achievement.* Knoxville: University of Tennessee Value-Added Research and Assessment Center.

Schmidt, F. (2004, March). 10,000 managers can't be wrong. *Gallup Management Journal.* Retrieved January 17, 2005, from http://gmj.gallup.com/content/default.asp?ci=10882

APPENDIX

The Clifton StrengthsFinder:

Research FAQs

The Gallup Organization

February 2005

Foreword

Many technical issues must be considered in the evaluation of an instrument such as the Clifton StrengthsFinder. One set of issues revolves around information technology and the expanding possibilities that Web-based applications offer for those who study human nature. Another set of issues involves what is known as psychometrics, which is the scientific study of human behavior through measurement. The Clifton StrengthsFinder is required to meet many American and international standards for psychometrics applied to test development (such as AERA/APA/NCME, 1999). The Clifton StrengthsFinder Research FAQs deal with some questions that emerge from those standards as well as technical questions that a leader may have about the use of the Clifton Strengths-Finder in his or her organization.

A few technical references have been cited for readers who wish to review primary source material. These technical materials may be found in local university libraries or on the Internet. The reader is encouraged to review the sources cited at the end of the FAQs. Readers with other research questions are encouraged to contact Gallup and request a copy of *The Clifton StrengthsFinder Technical Report: Development and Validation* (Lopez, Hodges, & Harter, 2005).

What is the Clifton StrengthsFinder?

The Clifton StrengthsFinder is a Web-based talent assess-ment instrument from the perspective of Positive Psycholo-gy. Through a secure connection, the Clifton StrengthsFind-er presents 180 items to the user. Each item lists a pair of potential self-descriptors, such as "I read instructions care-fully" and "I like to jump right into things." The descrip-tors are placed as if anchoring polar ends of a continuum. From each pair, the participant is then asked to choose the descriptor that best describes him or her, and also the extent to which it does so. The participant is given 20 seconds to respond to a given item before the system moves on to the next item. (Clifton StrengthsFinder developmental research showed that the 20-second limit resulted in a negligible item noncompletion rate.)

What is Positive Psychology?

For more than 50 years following World War II, psychol-ogy focused primarily on a pathology model, attempting to diagnose and treat mental illness. Research focused on re-pairing damage within a disease model of human function-ing. Although this period yielded many important break-throughs in the treatment of mental illness, psychology's predominant focus on the pathology model allowed for very little attention on the study of fulfilled individuals and thriving organizations. A search of more than 100 years of the psychology literature found approximately 8,000 articles on anger, 58,000 on anxiety, and 71,000 on depression, but only about 850 articles on joy, 3,000 on happiness, and 5,700 on life satisfaction turned up. Articles on negative emotions surpassed those on positive emotions by a 14-1 ratio (My-ers, 2000).

A new perspective in psychology, led by such pioneers as Donald O. Clifton, Ph.D., and Martin Seligman, Ph.D., is known as Positive Psychology. Positive Psychology is de-fined as "the scientific study of optimal human functioning. It aims to discover and promote the factors that allow indi-viduals and communities to thrive" (Sheldon, Fredrickson, Rathunde, & Csikszentmihalyi, 2000). Positive Psychology is about identifying the talents and strengths in individuals and organizations, and helping them develop and excel by building upon those talents and strengths. This new para-digm explores ways to help people flourish rather than sim-ply function. Topics receiving attention within the Positive Psychology movement include courage, strength, wisdom, spirituality, happiness, hope, resiliency, confidence, satis-faction, and other related areas of study. These topics are studied at the individual level or in a work group, family, or community. The strong reception to this positive approach to psychology is evidenced through special journal issues de-voted to Positive Psychology in the American Psychologist (January 2000, March 2001) and the Journal of Humanistic Psychology (Winter 2001), as well as a host of edited books on topics in the field of Positive Psychology (Cameron, Dut-ton, & Quinn, 2003; Keyes & Haidt, 2003; Linley & Joseph, 2004; Lopez & Snyder, 2003; Snyder & Lopez, 2002).

The Gallup Organization has been a prominent and recog-nized leader in the Positive Psychology movement since its inception. In January 2003, Dr. Clifton was award-ed an American Psychological Association Presidential

Commendation in recognition of his pioneering role in Strengths-Based Psychology. The commendation states, "Whereas, living out the vision that life and work could be about building what is best and highest, not just about correcting weaknesses, [Clifton] became the Father of Strengths-Based Psychology."

Gallup has sponsored and hosted the first five major Positive Psychology Summits, now attended annually by more than 300 research leaders, graduate students, and practitioners. Gallup is also actively involved in the science of Positive Psychology through theory development and empirical research in the areas of talent-based hiring, strengths-based development, employee engagement, and customer engagement. Further, many of the leading academics in the Positive Psychology field are members of Gallup's Senior Scientist program designed for global research leaders who teach at conferences and client programs, conduct publishable research, and lend their expertise to Gallup research design and consulting. Current Gallup Senior Scientists engaged in Positive Psychology research and instruction include Chip Anderson (Azusa Pacific University), Bruce Avolio (University of Nebraska-Lincoln), Mihaly Csikszentmihalyi (Claremont Graduate University), Ed Diener (University of Illinois-Urbana Champaign), Barbara Fredrickson (University of Michigan), Daniel Kahneman (Princeton University), Fred Luthans (University of Nebraska-Lincoln), and Phil Stone (Harvard University).

James K. Clifton, Gallup Chairman and CEO, articulated the following vision for the future of Positive Psychology in his letter to attendees of the First International Positive Psychology Summit.

> We believe many of the answers and solutions the world needs most lie within this new science [of Positive Psychology]. We [Gallup] will continue to do our part to contribute both financial and methodological resources to help harden with math and economics what many perceive to be a science that is too soft. They are of course, wrong, and have no idea of the power in many of the discoveries that you [Positive Psychological researchers] have made. The best partnership Gallup can have with this new institution is to help provide research and evidence that this science is as hard as physics or medicine. That will be our contribution (Clifton, 2002).

Is the Clifton StrengthsFinder supposed to be a work-related inventory, a clinical inventory, both, or neither?

The Clifton StrengthsFinder is an omnibus assessment based on Positive Psychology. Its primary application has been in the work domain, but it has been used for understanding individuals in a variety of roles and settings -- employees, executive teams, students, families, and personal development. It is *not* intended for clinical assessment or diagnosis of psychiatric disorders.

Why isn't the Clifton StrengthsFinder based on the "big five" factors of personality that have been well established in research journals since the 1980s?

The "big five" factors of personality are neuroticism (which reflects emotional stability -- reverse-scored), extroversion (seeking the company of others), openness (interest in new experiences, ideas, and so forth), agreeableness (likeability, harmoniousness), and conscientiousness (rule abidance, discipline, integrity). A substantial amount of scientific research has demonstrated that human personality functioning can be summarized in terms of these five dimensions. This research has been conducted across cultures and languages (for example, McCrae and Costa, 1987; McCrae, Costa, Lima, et al., 1999; McCrae, Costa, Ostendorf, et al., 2000).

The major reason that the Clifton StrengthsFinder is not based on the big five is that the big five is a measurement model rather than a conceptual one. It was derived from factor analysis. No theory underpinned it. It consists of the most generally agreed upon minimal number of personality factors, but conceptually it is no more correct than a model with four or six factors (Block, 1995; Hogan, Hogan, and Roberts, 1996). Some parts of the Clifton StrengthsFinder could be boiled down to aspects of the big five, but nothing would be gained from doing so. In fact, reducing the respondent's Clifton StrengthsFinder score to five dimensions would produce less information than is produced by any current measure of the big five, as those measures report subscores within those of the five major dimensions.

How was the Clifton StrengthsFinder developed?

The conceptual basis of the Clifton StrengthsFinder is grounded in more than three decades of the study of success across a wide variety of functions in business and education. Data from more than two million individuals were considered in the development of the Clifton Strengths-Finder. The item pairs were selected from a database of criterion-related validity studies, including more than 100 predictive validity studies (Schmidt & Rader, 1999). Factor and reliability analyses were conducted in multiple samples to assess the contribution of items to measurement of themes and the consistency and stability of theme scores -- thereby achieving the goal of a balance between maximized theme information and efficiency in instrument length.

Why does the Clifton StrengthsFinder use these 180 item pairs and not others?

These pairs reflect Gallup's research over three decades of studying successful people in a systematic, structured manner. They were derived from a quantitative review of item functioning, from a content review of the representativeness of themes and items within themes, with an eye toward the construct validity of the entire assessment. Given the breadth of talent we wish to assess, the pool of items is large and diverse. Well-known personality assessments range from 150 to upward of 400 items.

Are the Clifton StrengthsFinder items ipsatively scored, and if so, does this limit scoring of the items?

Ipsativity is a mathematical term that refers to an aspect of a data matrix, such as a set of scores. A data matrix is said to be ipsative when the sum of the scores for each respondent is a constant. More generally, ipsativity refers to a set of scores that define a person in particular but is comparable between persons in only a very limited way. For example, if you rank-ordered your favorite colors and someone else rank-ordered their favorite colors, one could not compare the *intensity* of preference for any particular color due to ipsativity; only the *ranking* could be compared. Of the 180 Clifton StrengthsFinder items, less than 30 percent are ipsatively scored. These items are distributed over the range of Clifton StrengthsFinder themes, and no one theme contains more than one item scored in a way that would produce an ipsative data matrix (Plake, 1999).

How are Clifton StrengthsFinder theme scores calculated?

Scores are calculated on the basis of the mean of the intensity of self-description. The respondent is given three response options for each self-description: strongly agree, agree, and neutral. A proprietary formula assigns a value to each response category. Values for items in the theme are averaged to derive a theme score. Scores can be reported as a mean, as a standard score, or as a percentile.

Was modern test score theory (for example, IRT) used to develop the Clifton StrengthsFinder?

The Clifton StrengthsFinder was developed to capitalize on the accumulated knowledge and experience of Gallup's talent-based strengths practice. Thus, items were initially chosen on the basis of traditional validity evidence (construct, content, criterion). This is a universally accepted method for developing assessments. Methods to apply IRT to

assessments that are both heterogeneous and homogeneous are only now being explored (for example, Waller,
Thompson, and Wenk, 2000). Further iterations of the Clifton StrengthsFinder may well use other statistical methods
to refine the instrument.

What construct validity research has been conducted in relation to the Clifton StrengthsFinder?

The Clifton StrengthsFinder is an omnibus assessment of
talents based on Positive Psychology. Therefore, it undoubtedly has correlational linkages to these measures to about
the same extent that personality measures link to other
measures in general.

Construct validity can be assessed through a number of
analysis types. During development phases, a number of
items were pilot tested. The items with the strongest psychometric properties (including item correlation to theme)
were retained.

Items should correlate to their proposed themes (constructs)
at a higher level than they do to other themes (constructs.)
In a follow-up study of 601,049 respondents, the average
item-to-proposed-theme correlation (corrected for part-
whole overlap) was 6.6 times larger than the average item
correlation to other themes.

Construct validity can also be assessed on the basis of convergent and discriminant validity evidence. A 2003 construct validity study explored the relationship between
the Clifton StrengthsFinder and the five-factor model of
personality. Several expected associations between Clifton
StrengthsFinder themes and five-factor model constructs

were found. For example, the Discipline theme correlates .81 with a measure of conscientiousness. Theoretically, these constructs have similar definition in relation to orderliness and planning. Other examples include the .83 correlation between Woo and extroversion, the .70 correlation between Ideation and intellectence, and the .58 correlation between Positivity and agreeableness.

Convergent and discriminant validity studies are a part of past and ongoing construct validity research.

Can Clifton StrengthsFinder scores change?

This is an important question for which there are both technical and conceptual answers.

Technical answers: The talents measured by Clifton Strengths-Finder are expected to demonstrate a property called reliability. Reliability has several definitions. The most important form of reliability estimate for the Clifton Strengths-Finder is technically known as test-retest reliability, which is the extent to which scores are stable over time. Test-retest reliabilities on the Clifton StrengthsFinder themes are high in relation to current psychometric standards.

Almost all Clifton StrengthsFinder themes have a test-retest reliability over a six-month interval between .60 and .80. A maximum test-retest reliability score of 1 would indicate that all Clifton StrengthsFinder respondents received *exactly* the same score over two assessments. The average correlation of an individual's theme ranking across multiple time periods is .74 (across 706 participants with an average of 17 months between administrations).

Conceptual answers: While an evaluation of the full extent of this stability is, of course, an empirical question, the conceptual origins of a person's talents are also relevant. Gallup has studied the life themes of top performers in an extensive series of research studies combining qualitative and quantitative investigations over many years. Participants have ranged from youths in their early teens to adults in their mid-seventies. In each of these studies, the focal point was the identification of long-standing patterns of thought, feeling, and behavior associated with success. The lines of interview questioning used were both prospective and retrospective, such as "What do you want to be doing ten years from now?" and "At what age did you make your first sale?" In other words, the timeframe of interest in our original studies of excellence in job performance was long term, not short term. Many of the items developed provided useful predictions of job stability, thereby suggesting that the measured attributes were of a persistent nature. Tracking studies of job performance over two- to three-year time spans added to the Gallup understanding of what it takes for a job incumbent to be consistently effective, rather than just achieve impressive short-term gains. The prominence of dimensions and items relating to motivation and to values in much of the original life themes research also informed the design of a Clifton StrengthsFinder instrument that can identify those enduring human qualities.

At this relatively early stage in the application of the Clifton StrengthsFinder, it is not yet clear how long an individual's salient features, so measured, will endure. In general, however, it is likely to be years rather than months. We may perhaps project a minimum of five years and upper ranges of 30 to 40 years and longer. There is growing evidence (for example, Judge, Higgins, Thoresen, and Barrick, 1999) that some aspects of personality are predictive throughout many decades of the life span. Some Clifton StrengthsFinder themes may turn out to be more enduring than others. Cross-sectional studies of different age groups will provide the earliest insights into possible age-related changes in normative patterns of behaviors. The first explanations for apparent changes in themes, as measured, should therefore be sought in the direction of measurement error rather than as indications of a true change in the underlying trait, emotion, or cognition. The respondents themselves should also be invited to offer an explanation for any apparent discrepancies.

How can one determine that the Clifton StrengthsFinder works?

The question of whether an assessment such as the Clifton StrengthsFinder "works" is addressed in an ongoing study of the construct validity of the instrument through psychometric and conceptual review. The Clifton StrengthsFinder is based on more than 30 years of evidence as to the nature of talents and the application of strengths analysis. This evidence was summarized in a recent scientific study that used meta-analysis (Schmidt & Rader, 1999).

The research literature in the behavioral and social sciences includes a multitude of individual studies with apparently conflicting conclusions. Meta-analysis allows the researcher to estimate the mean correlation between variables and make corrections for artifactual sources of variation in findings across studies. As such, it provides uniquely powerful information because it controls for measurement and

195

sampling errors and other idiosyncrasies that distort the results of individual studies. (More than one thousand meta-analyses have been published in the psychological, educational, behavioral, medical, and personnel selection fields.) For a detailed review of meta-analysis across a variety of fields, see Lipsey and Wilson (1993).

What is strengths-based development?

Identification of talent is critical to strengths-based development. A popular means for identifying talent is to consider an individual's top five areas of talent as indicated by responses to the Clifton StrengthsFinder, Gallup's online talent assessment instrument. Considering these top five areas ("themes") of talent, known as one's Signature Themes, can help individuals understand and, as a result, internalize the themes that offer their most natural talents.

Signature Themes are a useful resource in the identification of talent. One's spontaneous reactions to any situation are an important indicator of talents, and the ranking of themes presented in a Clifton StrengthsFinder report is based upon spontaneous, top-of-mind reactions to the paired descriptors presented by the instrument.

Yearnings, rapid learning, satisfactions, and timelessness should also be considered when identifying talents (Clifton & Nelson, 1992). Yearnings reveal the presence of a talent, particularly when they are felt early in life. A yearning can be described as a pull, a magnetic influence, which draws one to a particular activity or environment time and again. Rapid learning offers another trace of talent. In the context of a new challenge or a new environment, something sparks in individual's talent. Immediately their brain seems to light up as if a whole bank of switches were suddenly flicked to "on" -- and the speed at which they learn a new skill or gain new knowledge provides a telltale clue to the talent's presence and power. Satisfactions are psychological fulfillment that results when one takes on and successfully meets challenges that engage their greatest talents. Timelessness can also serve as a clue to talent. When individuals become so engrossed in an activity that they lose track of time, it may be because the activity engaged one of their talents.

Strengths-based development begins with the identification of talent, and continues as one integrates his or her talents into his or her view of self. Successful strengths-based development results in desired behavioral change (Clifton & Harter, 2003). Client-sponsored studies have provided evidence that strengths-based development relates to various positive outcomes, including increases in employee engagement and productivity.

Managers who create environments in which employees are able to make the most of their talents have more productive work units with less employee turnover (Clifton & Harter, 2003). Studies show that strengths-based development increases self-confidence, direction, hope, and altruism (Hodges & Clifton, 2004). Ongoing research continues to explore the impact of strengths-based development on desired outcomes.

How can the Clifton StrengthsFinder be administered, scored, and reported for individuals who are unable to use the Internet because of either disability or economic status?

In regard to economic status (a.k.a. the digital divide), possible solutions include accessing the Internet from a library or school. It should be noted that some organizations with which Gallup works do not have universal Internet access. In these cases, as with those from disadvantaged backgrounds, the solution generally has involved special access from a few central locations.

In regard to disability, a range of accommodations is available. Generally, the most effective is for the participant to request that the timer that governs the pace of the Clifton StrengthsFinder administration be turned off. This and other accommodations would need to be arranged with Gallup on a case-by-case basis in advance of taking the Clifton StrengthsFinder.

What is the recommended reading level for Clifton StrengthsFinder users? What alternatives are available for those who do not meet that level?

The Clifton StrengthsFinder is designed for completion by those with at least an eighth- to tenth-grade reading level (in most cases, those 14 years of age or older). Trials of the Clifton StrengthsFinder in our youth leadership studies have demonstrated neither significant nor consistent problems in completion of the Clifton StrengthsFinder by teens. Possible alternatives or accommodations include turning off the pace timer to allow time to consult a dictionary or otherwise seek the meaning of a word.

Is the Clifton StrengthsFinder appropriate across demographic groups, countries, and languages?

There is overwhelming evidence from both Gallup and other research organizations that the structure of talent and personality dimensions such as those measured by the Clifton StrengthsFinder and other instruments does not vary across cultures and nationalities.

For instance, the average item-to-theme correlation is quite similar across countries. The standard deviation of the correlations across countries is .026 and ranges from .01 to .04 across themes. Across languages, similar results were obtained, with an average standard deviation of the correlations across languages of .024 and range from .01 to .03. With regard to theme intercorrelations, the standard deviation across countries averaged .03 with range of .01 to .07 across the 561 theme intercorrelations. Across languages, the standard deviation averaged .02, with range from .01 to .06. In summary, the theme intercorrelations are stable across cultural contexts.

The Clifton StrengthsFinder has international presence as a talent measurement instrument. It is currently available in 17 languages, with several other translations planned for the future. More than 110,000 of the first one million respondents completed the Clifton StrengthsFinder in a language other than English. Clifton StrengthsFinder respondents have come from nearly 50 different countries. Twenty-five of these countries have had at least 1,000 respondents. More than 225,000 respondents report a country of residence other than the United States.

Research exploring the age of Clifton StrengthsFinder respondents has revealed that the average item-to-theme correlation is quite similar across age groups. Average standard deviation of the correlations is .02 and ranges from .00 to .09 across themes.

Research into the gender of Clifton StrengthsFinder respondents has revealed that the item-total correlations are similar and consistently positive. Differences in item-total correlations between genders range from .00 to .06 across themes.

What feedback does a respondent get from the Clifton StrengthsFinder?

Feedback varies in accordance with the reason the person completes the Clifton StrengthsFinder. Sometimes the respondent receives only a report listing his or her top five themes -- those in which the person received his or her highest scores. In other situations the person may also review the remaining 29 themes, along with action suggestions for each theme, in a personal feedback session with a Gallup consultant or in a supervised team-building session with their colleagues.

Theme combinations are rare and powerful. There are 278,256 possible unique combinations of Signature Themes, and 33.39 million different permutations with unique order can exist.

Since 1998, the Clifton StrengthsFinder has been used as Gallup's initial diagnostic tool in development programs with various academic institutions, faith-based organizations, major businesses, and other organizations. The Clifton

StrengthsFinder has been used to facilitate the development of individuals across hundreds of roles including: manager, customer service representative, salesperson, administrative assistant, nurse, lawyer, pastor, leader, student, teacher, and school administrator.

References

The following references are provided for readers interested in particular details of these FAQs. This reference list is not meant to be exhaustive, and although many of the references use advanced statistical techniques, the reader should not be deterred from reviewing them.

American Educational Research Association, American Psychological Association, National Council on Measurement in Education (AERA/APA/NCME). 1999. *Standards for educational and psychological testing*. Washington, D.C.: American Educational Research Association.

American Psychologist. Positive psychology [special issue]. 2000. Washington, D.C.: American Psychological Association.

Block, J. 1995. A contrarian view of the five-factor approach to personality description. *Psychological Bulletin* 117:187–215.

Cameron, K.S., Dutton, J.E., & Quinn, R.E. (Eds.). 2003. *Positive organizational scholarship*. San Francisco: Berrett-Koehler.

Clifton, D.O., & Harter, J.K. 2003. Strengths investment. In K.S. Cameron, J.E. Dutton, & R.E. Quinn (Eds.), *Positive organizational scholarship*. (pp. 111-121). San Francisco: Berrett-Koehler.

Clifton, D.O, & Nelson, P. 1992. Soar with your strengths. New York: Delacorte Press.

Clifton, J.K. 2002. Letter addressed to attendees of the first international Positive Psychology Summit, Washington, DC.

Hodges, T.D., & Clifton, D.O. 2004. Strengths-based development in practice. In A. Linley & S. Joseph (Eds.), *Handbook of positive psychology in practice*. Hoboken, New Jersey: John Wiley and Sons, Inc.

Hogan, R., J. Hogan, and B. W. Roberts. 1996. Personality measurement and employment decisions: Questions and answers. *American Psychologist* 51:469–77.

Hunter, J. E., and F. L. Schmidt. 1990. *Methods of meta-analysis: Correcting error and bias in research findings*. Newbury Park, CA: Sage.

Judge, T. A., C. A. Higgins, C. J. Thoresen, and M. R. Barrick. 1999. The big five personality traits, general mental ability, and career success across the life span. *Personnel Psychology* 52:621–52.

Keyes, C.L.M., & Haidt, J. (Eds.). 2003. *Flourishing: Positive psychology and the life well-lived*. Washington, DC.: APA.

Linley, A., & Joseph, S. (Eds.). 2004. *Positive psychology in practice*. Hoboken, NJ: John Wiley & Sons, Inc.

Lipsey, M. W., and D. B. Wilson. 1993. The efficacy of psychological, educational, and behavioral treatment. *American Psychologist* 48:1181–1209.

Lopez, S.J., Hodges, T.D., and Harter, J.K. 2005. The Clifton StrengthsFinder technical report: Development and validation. Princeton, NJ: The Gallup Organization.

Lopez, S.J., & Snyder, C.R. (Eds.). 2003. *Positive psychological assessment: A handbook of models and measures*. Washington, DC.: American Psychological Association.

McCrae, R. R., and P. T. Costa. 1987. Validation of the five-factor model of personality across instruments and observers. *Journal of Personality and Social Psychology* 52:81–90.

McCrae, R. R., P. T. Costa, M. P. de Lima, et al. 1999. Age differences in personality across the adult life span: Parallels in five cultures. *Developmental Psychology* 35:466–77.

McCrae, R. R., P. T. Costa, F. Ostendorf, et al. 2000. Nature over nurture: Temperament, personality, and life span development. *Journal of Personality and Social Psychology* 78:173–86.

Myers, D. 2000. The funds, friends, and faith of happy people. *American Psychologist*, 55: 56-67.

Plake, B. 1999. *An investigation of ipsativity and multicollinearity properties of the StrengthsFinder Instrument* [technical report]. Lincoln, NE: The Gallup Organization.

Schmidt, F.L., & Rader, M. 1999. Exploring the boundary conditions for interview validity: Meta-analytic validity findings for a new interview type. *Personnel Psychology*, 52: 445-464.

Sheldon, K., Fredrickson, B., Rathunde, K., & Csikszentmihalyi, M. 2000. Positive psychology manifesto (Rev. Ed.). Philadelphia. Retrieved May 1, 2003 from the World Wide Web: http://www.positivepsychology.org/akumalmanifesto.htm.

Snyder, C.R., & Lopez, S.J. (Eds.). 2002. *The handbook of positive psychology.* New York: Oxford University Press.

Waller, N. G., J. S. Thompson, and E. Wenk. 2000. Using IRT to separate measurement bias from true group differences on homogeneous and heterogeneous scales: An illustration with the MMPI. *Psychological Methods* 5:125–46.

Acknowledgements

No one has contributed more to this book than Dr. Donald O. Clifton. Don spent his life researching, conceptualizing, and inspiring teachers and the entire field of education. Some of his earliest work revolved around the study of great teachers, and until his last day, Don was passionate about strengths-based teaching. This book is a reality only because of his legacy, his mission, and his vision.

Very special thanks to our excellent and incredibly talented writing partner on this book, Jennifer Robison. Jen has a rare gift for storytelling and for making complex research come to life. She also has a great sense of humor. This book would not have been possible without her.

The foundation of this book was laid by a group of extremely talented teachers within Gallup's Education Division.

Dr. Gary Gordon, Gallup's education global practice leader, carries the torch of quality and excellence. His commitment to research, which is the underpinning for tools that teachers can use, is undaunted. He has contributed major components to the conceptual framework of this book.

JerLene Mosley, who is the consummate teacher, exudes joy in teaching and love of students. Kelly Peaks Horner's ability to transform schools into places where teachers can thrive is unparalled. And Ella Turrentine, whose combination of intelligence, values, and talent come together in a uniquely powerful way, was a great help. Key thought leaders about strengths in schools include Sherry Ehrlich and Connie Rath — two women who know about greatness in teaching.

Others who have contributed to the growth and impact of strengths in schools include Judy Bailey, Denise Hinkley, Gary

Evans, Dee Drozd, Irene Burklund, and Mark Pogue. They have our thanks and gratitude.

A critical portion of this book is in Chapter Four — the action items — to which Curt Liesveld contributed greatly. His depth of strengths understanding is unmatched. Sue Munn, an expert on strengths in teaching, was also a tremendous help with this chapter.

Paul Petters, Kelly Henry, and Mark Stiemann are world-class editors who contributed to the perfection of the words on these pages. Carolyn Madison is a first-rate leader of this editorial team. And Molly Hardin did a brilliant job designing the layout for this book.

Finally, without the executive direction of Geoff Brewer, Tom Rath, Piotrek Juszkiewicz, Larry Emond, and Jim Clifton, this book would have remained just a magnificent idea. Because of their vision, it has become what we hope is a magnificent reality for teachers everywhere.

Gallup Press exists to educate and inform the people who govern, manage, teach, and lead the world's six billion citizens. Each book meets The Gallup Organization's requirements of integrity, trust, and independence and is based on Gallup-approved science and research.